Advance Praise for *Half of a Whole*

"I cannot tell you how blown away I was by your memoir. Devoured it, actually. The characters are so real. And your honesty about yourself...the way you take the reader through those years of figuring it out...."

—Leslie Bedford

"I was in your skin, seeing what you saw, feeling what you felt...unadorned, direct, very real and compelling storytelling, but with insight and such intelligence...."

—Joan Kavanaugh

"I thought I would read it at a later time but sat down and read it from beginning to end...not until I got near the ending chapters could I see the full impact of purpose in the writing, its depth and extent, and the title in full bloom."

—Marian Ecklund

"I could not stop reading your words. Your story is both beautiful and devastating."

—Laura Flint

"I couldn't put it down! Very powerful. Your journey was intense. I cried with each loss."

—Cindy Barham

T0036287

HALF OF A WHOLE

My Fight for a Separate Life

Marilyn Peterson Haus

Post Hill
PRESS

A POST HILL PRESS BOOK
ISBN: 978-1-64293-934-7
ISBN (eBook): 978-1-64293-935-4

Half of a Whole:
My Fight for a Separate Life
© 2021 by Marilyn Peterson Haus
All Rights Reserved

Permissions: Ainslie, R. C. *The Psychology of Twinship*. Northvale, NJ: Jason Aronson, 1997. Excerpt used by permission from the author.

Cover art by Cody Corcoran; concept by Naomi Haus-Roth

This is a work of nonfiction. All people, locations, events, and situations are portrayed to the best of the author's memory.

No part of this book may be reproduced, stored in a retrieval system, or transmitted by any means without the written permission of the author and publisher.

Post Hill Press
New York • Nashville
posthillpress.com

Published in the United States of America
10

Dedication

for my twin
and my mother

There are early, strong ties between twins, ties that foster mutual interidentification between them and serve to cement the twinship psychologically for each twin. In this manner twins become primary actors in each other's emotional lives beginning early in their infancy.
The Psychology of Twinship, Ricardo Ainslie

And Isaac loved Esau…but Rebekah loved Jacob.
Genesis 25:28 (KJV)

CONTENTS

AUTHOR'S NOTE

While writing this book, I relied on a trove of material that I had collected over the decades—stacks of long and detailed letters my mother wrote; my twin's and my baby books, in which she recorded our early years; the family histories she wrote; boxes and drawers packed with documents I saved; my school yearbooks; scrapbooks I made; genealogical studies, undertaken by my relatives; descriptions of my dreams, as I recorded them at the time; and research I undertook to better understand the past.

To recreate the characters, conversations, and events, I relied on my memory, old family photographs, and the stories we told. At times, I consulted with my siblings, cousins, and classmates to refresh my memory.

The names of the characters are as they were at the time.

CHAPTER 1

The admitting nurse thought I was an idiot. I could see it in her eyes. "What took you so long?" she asked, peering over the top of her reading glasses. "We've been waiting—it's been hours since you called!" Sharon sank into her gold corduroy jacket. My hands trembled in my lap.

What took so long? If the nurse had seen me shaking outside Mom's condominium on the frigid Minnesota morning, if she had heard the officer shouting—"Try to make it easy for him, and what does he do? Fights like a bull! Has to trash the place!"—if she had seen him spraying spit in my face as he ranted—"Kicks his way down the hallway! Shatters the glass door with his stocking feet!"—if she had heard me pleading with him to bring my brother to the emergency room, she wouldn't have looked at me the way she did.

"It took six attendants to get him on the gurney," the nurse said, leveling her gaze at me. "The first set of shots didn't touch him. Had to give him a second round to bring him down."

I had no idea my twin was so strong. He had never gotten into fights. At least none that I knew about.

My knuckles had turned a bloodless yellow. I unclenched my hands and wiggled my fingers while the nurse moved her pen down the admitting form. Sharon shoved her permed ash-blond hair away from her glasses, left me to do all the talking about her husband.

"He's forty-five years old," the nurse said, noting the date, October 29, 1941, when we were born. "It's highly unusual that he's never been hospitalized. The first manic episode normally occurs in the early twenties."

She stared at my stunned face. I stared back.

"Are there any people in your family who are manic-depressive?" she asked.

"No. Everyone in our family is fine."

She set the clipboard down and removed her glasses.

"This type of mental illness is very difficult to diagnose. If there's any history, any people in your family—maybe an aunt or an uncle—information like that could help us determine what's going on with your brother."

The nurse watched me as I opened and closed my hands, rubbed my knuckles. I wanted to tell her how Dr. Dowswell had never heard a second heartbeat; how Mom had said "I told you so!" after she gave birth to my twin; how Dad's face had broken into a proud grin in the picture she took with her Brownie box camera, one baby on each knee. Marilyn and Marvin. A girl, and finally, after waiting so many years, the boy he had wanted. But the nurse wouldn't care about any of that.

"I remember one time when Marvin seemed nervous," I said.

"What do you mean by 'nervous'?" she asked, squinting at me through her glasses.

"Nothing. Just that he seemed tense." I wanted to stop talking, but she kept staring at me. "He was on leave from Germany and came to visit George and me. We were living in Connecticut—we'd only been married a couple of months." I remembered how his eyes had flashed with anger, his pale face turning a deep red as he pounded the table while arguing with the long-distance operator. "It wasn't like him," I told the nurse, "talking to the operator like that."

"Go on," she said, as she scrawled notes on the form.

Years later, Mom had told me about the rest of his leave, which he spent with them, how Pastor Folden had driven to their farm to tell her he thought Marvin should see a doctor. I asked her what caused Pastor Folden to make such a shocking suggestion.

"Well, anyone could see that Marvin was nervous," she said, swatting her curly red hair away from her face. "I told Elsie what the minister said—she said Pastor Folden should be taken out and shot!"

I never dared to bring up the subject again.

I didn't bring it up with the nurse. She would have made too much of it. I did tell her about the scar on his arm, how it had always bothered me. One time I asked him about the thick, jagged mark. He said, "I got it in the military." I asked if he'd been in a fight, but he clammed right up. I knew better than to ask again.

"That's all I can think of," I said to the nurse.

She turned to Sharon.

"Anything come to mind?"

"No, I can't think of anything."

Sharon didn't mention the night, six years earlier, when they were at the farm for Dad's funeral. The rest of us had hovered over him in his hospital bed, but Marvin sat at the side of the room, not saying anything, as our father lay dying.

After the burial, I heard Marvin cry out in the middle of the night. Sharon was sleeping beside him. She had to have heard the anguish in his voice as it echoed through the silent house.

I never told anyone about it, except my husband, George. He had slept through it.

"How about depression?" the nurse asked, tapping her pen on the clipboard. "Any signs of depression in your family?"

The back of the chair was digging into my spine. I shifted my position before responding.

"I remember once when Dad had what I suppose could be called a bout of depression. It was at the time George and I got married."

I had been annoyed at his griping about having to wear a tuxedo instead of his "good enough" gray Sunday suit and his grumbling about my having someone from Augsburg College play Handel and Mendelssohn when our church organist could play some "perfectly fine" gospel hymns.

"Just ignore him," Mom said, "he'll get over it."

But it was hard to ignore my father when I had wanted him to enjoy the most important day in my life.

"It was perfectly understandable," I told the nurse. "Marvin had volunteered for the army, and Dad was upset because that meant he didn't want to take over the family farm. And not only that, his mother had died a couple of months before our wedding, so he had a lot on his mind."

"Go on," the nurse said, her pen scribbling across the clipboard.

"He told me he couldn't get to sleep at night. When I asked what was keeping him awake, he said he could hear his heart beating. I thought that was a strange reason for not being able to sleep. He ended up going to the doctor. Farmers never go to the doctor. He got some pills. Sleeping pills, I think."

"What else?" she asked.

"It was all for good reason. He did have a habit of worrying about the crops, but farmers always worry about the crops, and anyway, nothing ever kept him from getting his work done."

She clamped another sheet of paper onto her clipboard.

"I could be wrong about all of this," I said. "If you asked someone in our family, they'd say I was making it up."

There had been times when I was afraid to talk to Dad. Instead of being excited about a vacation, he was silent while lugging the milking machines from cow to cow. Sometimes, after we finished supper, he'd stand on the porch, saying nothing as he stared off into the distance. His silences only lasted a week or two, but I had feared they'd go on forever.

I didn't tell the nurse about his silences. She'd turn it into more than it was.

"What else?" she asked.

I thought about Marvin's tics and shrugs while we were growing up; the way Mom had to practically drag him out of bed so he'd be ready in time to catch the bus; the times he moped around the house, laying across his bed, when Dad wanted him to help with the work. No need to mention any of that. Lots of teenaged boys behaved that way.

"I can't think of anything more," I said. "Mom never gets depressed. She likes to complain if someone does something she doesn't like. She can go on for days, sometimes weeks, once she gets herself going."

"How about signs of depression with your relatives? Any aunts or uncles? Cousins?"

"Hard to tell." I massaged a muscle that had tightened up in the back of my neck. "There could be some depression. I can't know for sure. Swedes don't like to admit to anything being wrong. A manic Swede should be pretty easy to notice!"

Why was I making a stupid joke when my brother was in the emergency room, strapped down on a gurney, shot up with two rounds of God knows what? Maybe the nurse thought *I* was manic, running my mouth, shifting in my chair. Sometimes I wondered if I talked too much, especially around my relatives, filling in the gaps in the conversation as they sat, poker-faced, considering whether there was something they might like to say. At times I had a lot of energy. Maybe too much energy.

The nurse reached for the phone on the corner of her desk and punched four buttons. "He's been moved to a room," she said, as she dropped the receiver back into its cradle. "Would you like to see him?"

"Yes, I would like that," Sharon said. She reached down and picked up her purse and mittens.

Going to see my brother would have been the right thing to do. To try to explain why I had called the police. Reassure him that everything was going to be okay. But instead of going to face him, I hunched down in a chair and waited in the lobby.

What had gone wrong? What had happened to my brother?

CHAPTER 2

It was the wind, Mom said, that made her go into labor a month early. That, and the thirteen pairs of reeking overalls piled up outside the basement door. Dad and one of his brothers had shot a family of skunks, a dozen of them, that had taken up residence in a ramshackle house on a piece of land he had bought.

The way Mom told the story, she had plugged in her Maytag washing machine and filled it with rainwater from the cistern. After feeding the clothes through the wringer and into the metal washtubs, she hoisted the tubs, one by one, up the steep basement stairway and clothespinned a week's worth of laundry, including the thirteen pairs of overalls, onto the lines behind our house. But before the clothes had time to dry, a late-October storm raged in from the plains, howling through the flat prairie land of west-central Minnesota.

I imagined her red hair flying in the wind as she pressed the frozen clothes, stiff as boards, into the washtubs and carried them back into the basement, where she pinned them onto the clotheslines Dad had strung across the ceiling beams. After preparing supper, she lifted four-year-old Betty into her crib in their bedroom, scrubbed the pots and pans, and collapsed into bed.

At 3:00 a.m., she jiggled Dad.

"Winston. Wake up. It's time to go to the hospital."

"He was in no hurry," she said, shaking her head. He had tended to the birthing of many calves and knew these things took time. He stoked the coal in their Monarch range and brewed a fresh pot of coffee while she scurried about the bedroom, packing her clothes into their black cardboard suitcase and toweling up the trail of waters she left behind.

When Dad finished his second cup of coffee, he cranked the handle of their wooden telephone several vigorous rounds and waited for the operator to pick up, knowing the half dozen farmers on the party line would rush from their beds to rubberneck as he asked her to ring Dr. Dowswell. Unlike Betty, this baby was to be born in a hospital, as one had recently been constructed in the town of Willmar.

Dad braced Mom's arm as she stepped onto the running board of their 1938 Ford, easing her into the front seat, Betty between them. As Dad drove across the gravel road to his parents' house, Mom told Betty she would be staying with her Grandpa and Grandma Peterson while Mommy went to the hospital to get a "brand-new baby."

With Grandma nearly deaf, it had made no sense for Grandpa to waste good money on a telephone, so Dad woke him by pounding on the door. After transferring Betty into his father's lanky arms, he drove fourteen miles, past pastures, fields, and fences, to the new hospital.

Dad had grown impatient while waiting for Mom to produce a son. His mother had also tired of the long wait. "Well, Ruby, isn't it about time for you to have another one?" she asked, planting one hand on her hip as she looked up at Mom, who towered over her short, sturdy frame. Two months later, Dr. Dowswell confirmed the pregnancy Mom had suspected while Grandma was shaking a finger at her.

Everyone was thrilled.

Mom took note of the excessive amount of commotion inside her rapidly expanding belly. She told Dr. Dowswell she thought she might be carrying twins, but he never was able detect a second heartbeat as he slid his stethoscope back and forth across her belly.

"Weigh her again," he said, when the nurse reported my weight as five pounds, four and a half ounces. "She's got to weigh more than that."

The nurse placed me on the scale a second time.

"Well, that's as much as I can get her to weigh."

Mom always smiled when she came to this part, her favorite part, of the story.

Dr. Dowswell walked over to her and palpated her belly.

"Ah. There's another one in there."

"I told you so!" she said.

He grinned as the nurse weighed my brother in at five pounds, fifteen ounces.

"I have to hurry and find Winston," Dr. Dowswell said, "so I can tell him he got his boy!"

Mom had already addressed the birth announcements, crowding three stamps—a one-and-a-half-cent stamp, a one-cent stamp, and a half-cent stamp—onto the small, square envelopes. On the first line, she wrote "Mr. and Mrs. Winston G. Peterson." She had told Dad it was his job to fill in the remaining lines after the baby was born. On the second line, he wrote, "twin girl and boy," as they had not picked out matching names because he also had refused to believe her when she said she was carrying twins. On the third line he wrote "October 29," seeing no need to add "1941" as everyone already knew the year. On the last line he rounded our weights to "5½ – 6 pounds." Close enough, he figured, and easier to squeeze into the small space.

The next day, he mailed the announcements in Kerkhoven, the nearest town, seven miles away. Even so, most of our relatives had already heard the news. KWLM, the Willmar radio station, had announced our birth two hours after we were born.

After naming "his boy" Marvin, he told Mom it was her job to find a matching name for "her girl." She suggested many before he approved of the name Marilyn. In keeping with his approach, she gave me her given name, Ruby, as my middle name. "Marvin Winston" and "Marilyn Ruby."

Matching names for matching babies.

Dad took Grandma Peterson and Betty with him when, after the usual stay of nine days, he came to bring us home from the hospital.

Mom held one of "the twins" in her lap on the drive back. Grandma held the other.

Several men were drinking coffee at the table when Mom stepped into the kitchen. Dad had neglected to tell her he was having a milking machine installed in the barn, as REA, the Rural Electrification Administration, had brought electricity to their area a few months earlier.

A stream of relatives and friends arrived. They tiptoed behind Mom into the bedroom. "How can you tell them apart?" they asked, as they peered at the two blue-eyed, bald-headed babies lying side by side in their buggies.

When the hospital bill for forty-five dollars arrived in our mailbox, Dad paid it immediately. He offered to pay Dr. Dowswell double his usual fee of twenty-five dollars.

"There is no need to pay extra," Dr. Dowswell said. "Delivering two babies was hardly any more work than if there had only been one."

Dad grinned. Two for the price of one.

He thought he had gotten a bargain.

CHAPTER 3

More than once, Dad had scowled, running his thick fingers through his coffee-colored hair, as he told Marvin to stay away from his tools. But on a hot summer day, the allure of monkey wrenches and needle-nose pliers strewn across his workbench in the machine shed proved to be too enticing for an eight-year-old boy to resist. He clamped a chunk of wood in the jaws of the bench vice and scraped a rasp across it, while I sketched Tweety Bird in the thick layer of dust powdering the dirt floor with my big toe. After poking through a can of nuts and washers, he rummaged through the boards Dad had stockpiled between the studs of the corrugated steel walls. At the far corner, he wedged himself behind a pair of stacked sawhorses.

"Marilyn, come quick! See what I found!"

I swatted the cobwebs away from my face as I squeezed into the dimly lit space. "Ooh, baby banties. Aren't they cute?" I said, stroking the tiny balls of fluff with the tip of my finger. "Where do you think their mother went?"

"Maybe she's out hunting for something to eat," Marvin said, his white hair tufted up in a cowlick on his forehead, big blue eyes sparkling with pride at his find.

"I wonder why the other eggs didn't hatch," I said, counting five chicks nestled on top of six blue-green eggs. "They must not be any good."

He slipped his hand under the chicks and pulled out one of the unhatched eggs. After stepping outside, he raised his arm high and slammed the egg to the ground. A curled-up chick splashed out of the shell. I bent down to study the scrawny body, wet with slime, eyes too big for its head.

"What do you think was wrong with it?" I asked.

"How should I know?" he said with a shrug.

He lifted another egg from the nest and hurled it to the ground. A second chick spilled out. Soon six curled-up chicks lay splattered in the dirt.

Mom happened to walk by, carrying two pails of feed for the chicks in the brooder house. She paid little attention to us as we searched for pullet eggs in the woods, played with the baby mice in our granary, or pulled our fingers through the water in the cows' water tank to screen out the spongy moss. But she stopped when she saw the broken shells.

"Why did you break the bantam's eggs? If you had left them alone, they would have hatched! And how many times does your dad have to tell you to stay away from the machine shed?"

My stomach lumped up in a knot. I had thought all eggs hatched at the same time. We hadn't meant to kill the bantam's chicks. We liked to follow the small black-and-brown hens while their chicks scurried behind them as they searched for kernels of grain by the corncribs and watch them flutter their wings as they rushed to gobble up the bugs and seeds the hens ripped up with their spiked claws. But most of the chicks would vanish before the summer ended.

"What happens to them?" I once asked Dad when a hen had only one chick left.

"Bantams are hard to raise," he had said, twisting his mouth to the side while shaking his head. "We don't have much luck with them. Besides, they're just for decoration."

After Mom picked up her pails and continued to the brooder house, I followed Marvin into the woods behind the machine shed. The dirt felt crumbly between my toes, the shade of the trees cool on my back.

Marvin didn't worry about killing the chicks, but my stomach felt sick.

When Mom got upset with me, I would hide inside a thicket of branches in the woods, wrapping my arms around my legs while deciding which gravel road to take when I ran away. Not the one that went west at the crossroad beside our place, because that road went too far, past the Black Hills, where Dad drove us on a vacation. I could go the opposite way on the same road, but in one mile I would pass our neighbor's place. If they saw me walking by, they'd crank four short rings on our party line and ask Mom if she knew where I was headed. I'd never walk north on the road that ran north and south, because that road passed by Monson Lake, where Dad once pointed at two shallow cellars in the tall grass as he told us about the thirteen people, mostly children, who had been killed by tomahawks.

The only road I could take was the one going south. South was the way Mom went when she drove to the Gamble Store in Kerkhoven each week to buy groceries. She always brought two comic books home, one for Marvin and one for me. We would hurry up to his room and stretch ourselves across his bed, where he laughed so hard at Elmer Fudd—"Be vewy vewy quiet. I'm hunting wabbits!"—that I laughed at him. But if I ran away on the road going south, I'd come to a crossroad after every mile, and I wouldn't know which turn to take because all the gravel roads looked alike—fields in all directions, an occasional wood with a house and barn, dogs that curled their lips and snarled.

I could stay hidden in the woods, but wolves might come after me during the night. Kidnappers, like the ones that snatched the Lindbergh boy, might be lurking among the trees, or scary creatures that I couldn't see, prowling in the dark.

When I felt like crying, I hid under Betty's and my bed. But my shirt would get stuck in the coils of the spring, the air would become hot and sticky, and I'd have trouble getting my breath. One time, Betty grabbed my foot and yanked me out. She wouldn't let me go until I told her what was wrong.

"Nobody loves me!" I said, gasping the words out.

She stared at my red, swollen eyes, her honey-colored curls fluffing out beside her bangs, before disappearing down the stairway.

"Mom says to tell you that everyone loves you," she had said when she returned, "and it's time for you to come down and get something to eat."

But this time, I didn't feel like running away. I followed Marvin farther into the woods, until we came to the old plow Dad's grandfather had used to break up the prairie sod. Marvin grabbed the wooden handles and shouted "Giddy-up! Giddy-up!" as he flicked his imaginary reins on his imaginary horses. He stepped over a rotting log and peed an arc that puddled two feet in front of us while I yanked down my shorts and squatted at his side.

Earlier that summer, I had sneaked a red bandana handkerchief from Dad's drawer in their bedroom while Mom was putting the discs she had scrubbed back into the cream separator in the barn. I rolled it into a sausage and pinned it to the front of my underpants.

"What are you doing with Dad's handkerchief?" Marvin asked as I stood beside him, holding the handkerchief and making peeing sounds.

A few days later, after I tired of wearing the handkerchief, I had tiptoed into their bedroom and put it back in Dad's drawer.

"I'm sick of playing in the woods," I said, hiking up my shorts. "Let's go jump in the quicksand. I called first!"

With Marvin two steps behind me, I ran to the old granary, climbed the wooden ladder, and leaped into the middle of a bin. *Thunk.* I sank up to my chest in the cool, slippery flax. *Thunk.* Marvin landed beside me. "Help! Help! I'm sinking in quicksand!" he shouted, as the weight of the flax paralyzed our legs. After thrashing our way to the side of the bin, we jumped again and again, until we heard Dad turn his tractor into our driveway for our noontime meal.

"Dinner is ready!" Mom shouted from the side porch of our white, square, two-story house with a pyramid-shaped roof and a long porch running across the front.

"Do you think Mom is still mad at us?" I asked, as we stepped down the ladder.

"What should she be mad about? Let's go eat. I'm hungry!"

After gulping our last swallows of milk, Marvin and I raced outside, the screen door banging behind us. He ran to the machine shed to grab the fork Dad used for digging potatoes. I met him at the side of the steer shed, where we found long, fat angleworms for Uncle Chester, Dad's youngest brother, when he wanted to go fishing.

I felt sorry for Chester because he had diabetes and wasn't allowed to eat the pies and cakes Mom baked, although he sometimes sneaked molasses crinkle cookies from our cookie jar. I wondered if diabetes was the reason he hadn't grown very tall, although he was taller than Grandma, who claimed to be five feet, but no one believed her.

Marvin stomped the fork deep into the ground and tipped it back, popping a large clod of black dirt out from under the long grass. I grabbed the ends of the worms and tugged them out, pulling carefully so I didn't break them into two pieces. If a pointed end disappeared into the dirt before I had time to snatch the worm, I crumbled the clod through my fingers until I found it. Sometimes we collected four or five worms in one forkful of dirt.

"Do you think worms can see?" I asked, studying the one in my palm. "Look at the way it waves its pointy end back and forth, like it's looking around."

"How could they see?" Marvin said, shrugging his shoulders. "They don't have eyes."

After we brought the can of worms across the road to Chester, who lived in the retirement house with Grandpa and Grandma Peterson, Marvin ran behind me to our haymow, where we climbed to the top of the hay.

"Watch me fly," I said, as I spread my arms and leaped, soaring through the air like the barn swallows that roosted in the rafters high above our heads.

"Watch me!" Marvin said, landing beside me in a mound of straw piled up on the floor.

We lay on our backs and watched the swallows flit from beam to beam. The haymow smelled sweet, like freshly cut alfalfa. Spindly grasshoppers played hopscotch in the hay. A beam of sunlight lit up a column of dust that glistened from the window at the peak of the roof to the spot where the light puddled on the floor.

"Do you think Mom is still mad at us for breaking the eggs?" I asked.

"Are you still worried about that?" he said.

He was able to toss aside things that bothered me. "Where do you think you're going to go?" he would ask when I wanted to run away.

We had always been together. How could I run away if he wouldn't go with me?

CHAPTER 4

*M*arvin chose the ones with stripes because they looked like tigers. I liked the ones with spots, one eye fringed by black, the other by white. But most of our barn cats, a dozen or so, were mouse-gray. We spied on them as they slept in a tangle of furry bodies behind the cows' stanchions where they stayed warm during the winter. In the summer, we stepped over them, stretched out like rubber bands to cool their bellies. They crowded around their dishes, like the blades of a fan, while Dad filled them with milk from a milking canister. They never were taken to a vet, never got vaccinated. The tomcats had scars on their faces, chunks missing from their ears. Some got run over while crossing the road. A few were eaten by coyotes and foxes. The ones that came down with distemper, which we knew as "cat sickness," looked wretched and never got well. They also disappeared.

Once Marvin held a cat upside down and dropped it so I could see how it could turn its body fast enough to land on its feet. Another time, we sneaked up on a pile of cats sleeping in the barn and shouted "BOO!" Cats flying. Cats landing on stretched out legs. Cats licking their paws, as if nothing had happened.

"That cat sure does know how to hunt," Dad said, scratching his head the day Mama Cat walked by, dragging three gophers in her mouth. Marvin and I lay on our bellies and watched her swat the other cats away until her kittens had eaten their fill. They hissed and growled as they gnawed the gophers' guts, their favorite snack. But they never scratched Marvin and me. We had tamed them when they were kittens.

Marvin and I were dragging stalks of straws in circles in the hay-mow, kittens tumbling after them, when I asked, "Do you remember that batch of kittens I found, the brand-new ones that disappeared?"

"What about them?"

"Remember how I asked Mom if she knew what happened to them?"

"What did she say?"

"She said, 'You'll have to ask your dad.'"

"What did he say?"

"He said cats shouldn't have kittens in the fall because the winters are too cold, and they'll get sick."

"What's wrong with that?" Marvin said, as a kitten captured the straw he had been circling in front of it.

"Well, what do you suppose happened to them?"

"Maybe a tomcat got them."

"Do you think our big, soft Tom Cat goes off and kills kittens at someone else's farm?"

"I don't know. Maybe they like to find other tomcats so they can fight. Can't you think about something else?"

But I couldn't put the thought of a tomcat killing little kittens out of my mind. Nor could I understand why the biggest piglets pushed the littlest ones away, drinking from two teats and leaving the weaker ones with none. And why were hens so cruel, pecking the ones that already had bloodied tails?

Marvin never worried about the kittens or the piglets or the bloodied hens. We had other differences as well. I moved fast and liked to try new things. He took more time to make up his mind and didn't like things to change. Even so, we played together from when we got up in the morning until it was time to go to bed.

I did not understand why the Old Testament twins, Esau and Jacob, couldn't get along. Why would Jacob trick their father, Isaac, into giving him the birthright that belonged to Esau, the firstborn son? Marvin and I never tried to trick Mom and Dad. We shared our comic books and our toys, and if we had only one candy bar, we found a knife and sliced it in half. And how could Jacob fool Isaac into giving him the blessing meant for Esau by covering his arms with the skins of baby goats to make them feel like Esau's hairy arms? Marvin and I had petted our neighbor's baby goats, and their fur didn't feel anything like the fuzzy hair on Dad's arms.

Marvin had tired of playing with the kittens. After stepping over the swarms of flies circling the splashes of cream on the cooler-room floor, we hopped down the crumbling stone steps that led to the long row of stanchions for our dozen Holstein cows.

We liked to follow Dad when he fed the cows. Sunlight filtered in through the cobwebs in the small windows as the cows lifted their heads while he pitched hay into their mangers. They twitched their ears as they slurped water from their water cups. The milking cups made a whooshing sound when Dad slipped them onto their teats.

"What do you think cows think about?" I asked Marvin, when a cow swung her big head around and focused her dark eyes on us.

"I don't know. What makes you think cows think?"

Marvin didn't wonder how a cow might see the world; he wondered how an auger could lift grain up a tube.

One evening while he was doing chores, Dad had said, "Put your hand here," as he pointed at a bump on a cow's fat belly. "Do you feel anything?"

"I feel something hard," Marvin said.

"I feel something inside her stomach pushing my hand," I said.

"It's a calf," Dad said, grinning at our astonished faces.

I wondered how the calf had gotten into the cow's belly and how it was going to get out.

Whenever a cow was about to have a calf, Dad would say "It's time for you to go to the house" because Mom thought watching a calf being born would make Betty and me afraid of having a baby. I obeyed Dad, but I was jealous of Marvin because he got to stay in the barn and watch.

Dad would take both Marvin and me along when he retrieved a new calf from the pasture. We would run to the two-wheeled trailer and climb over its low sides, bouncing against each other as we bumped our way to the small grove of trees where the heifer, a young cow, had hidden her calf. He stroked her side, talking to her in his deep, calm voice, before he hoisted her calf into the trailer with Marvin and me.

"Look how scared she is," I said as a heifer bellowed, her swollen udder swinging from side to side as she ran behind the trailer. "If she tries to jump in with her calf, we'll get smashed!"

"Don't worry," Marvin said. "If she gets too close, Dad will speed up."

"But I'm really scared. What if she attacks him?"

"Why would she attack him? She's just trying to get to her calf."

"She might think he's stealing it."

"He's not stealing it. He's just bringing it home."

"But the heifer doesn't know that!"

Dad propped the calf on its splayed legs in front of the barn door and waited for the heifer to stop running back and forth. After walking up to sniff her calf, she followed Dad as he carried it into the barn. Only then, after he had guided the calf's mouth to her teats, had my heart stopped pounding.

"I'm hungry," Marvin said, as we stepped out of the barn, squinting in the glistening rays of the midsummer sun. A row of barn swallows, their long, forked tails a glossy blue, perched like sentinels on the lines above our heads. A scattering of purple martins watched us from the steel skeleton of the windmill, its blades glinting in the sunlight, as Marvin followed me to the house.

But Mom was not in the kitchen ironing Dad's white shirts, nor was she peeling potatoes or kneading dough. We found Betty in the dining room, laying out a pattern for a gathered skirt, but Mom was not at her sewing machine stitching long patches on the knees of Dad's overalls. She wasn't in the living room, where her mother, Grandma Johnson, sat in a rocking chair, her crochet hook flashing in and out of a doily. Grandpa Johnson looked up from a church bulletin and said, "I don't know ver she vent," in his Swedish brogue that made Marvin and me giggle. We thought Mom's parents were ancient, the skin on their faces scrunched up into thick wrinkles, Grandpa walking slowly, Grandma clunking her cane across the floor.

"Mom, are you down there?" I shouted, peering down the stairway to the basement. But it wasn't Monday, and she wasn't washing clothes.

"Let's go check in the garden," Marvin said.

We hopped across the gravel road and around the clods of dirt in the field and found her swatting mosquitoes while twisting shiny fat tomatoes from their vines. After jumping over the rows of beans and carrots, we came to a long row of peas.

Neither Marvin nor I spoke as we tugged the swollen pods from the plants. I could tell he was happy by the way he tipped his head back and popped the peas into his mouth and by the arc of his arm as he flung the shells as far as he could make them fly. We seldom had much to say as we bent our heads together while poking the squishiness of a toad's belly, or as I examined the striations of a garter snake draped over the stick he held.

When Mom couldn't pile any more tomatoes into the milk pail, she lifted it into the red Radio Flyer wagon, next to the pail she had filled with green beans. She snapped the tops off an armload of beets and handed the leaves to us.

"Here, you can go feed these to the pigs."

On our way to the pigpen, Marvin stopped by the old steel-wheeled McCormick-Deering tractor that had been used to run the threshing machine.

He loved when Dad told him how the driveshaft on a power take-off transferred its power to a baler or how a corn elevator lifted cobs up to the opening in the roof of a corncrib. When we found him lying next to the corn planter or under the combine, Marvin would stop to watch.

"What are you fixing?" he would ask.

Dad mumbled an answer as he ratcheted his wrench around a nut.
"How did it get broken?"

Dad's answer was muffled as he reached for the grease gun.

"What part does that belt run?"

Dad was patient as he answered Marvin's string of questions. But I remembered the Sunday afternoon when we were playing with our cousins and Marvin yanked the crank of the steel-wheeled tractor several rounds. The engine burst into a clatter, shocking him as well as the rest of us when it started. Dad had dashed from the house, terrified one of us might fall beneath its wheels.

"You better not fool with it," I said, as Marvin flung his beet tops on the ground and climbed onto the metal seat of the tractor.

"I'm not going to start it. I'm just going to pretend I'm driving it."

"You'll get in trouble if Dad finds out."

"How will he find out? He's out in the field." He jammed in the clutch. "Vroom! Vroom! Vroom!"

I did not understand why he would play on the tractor after Dad had told him to stay away from it. Dad never spanked us, but I could hear the anger in his voice when Marvin ignored his warnings. I saw how his rage was building as he got Marvin out of bed each night and walked him into the bathroom, when his attempts to help him didn't stop the bedwetting. I wanted to meld my body with Marvin's to protect him from the heat of Dad's anger. But I couldn't keep him from wetting the bed, and I couldn't stop him from climbing on the tractor.

"Come on," I said, "let's go feed the pigs before Dad comes home and sees you."

He clambered down from the seat of the tractor, picked up his clump of beet tops, and followed me down the slope to the pigpen.

"Here pig! Here pig!" we shouted. A stampede of pigs scrambled out of their ruts in the cool black dirt. They screeched and jostled in their fight to be first, shoving the round flat ends of their snouts between the boards of the wooden fence to yank the beet tops out of our hands.

"Feel his nose," I said, sliding my finger around the rim of one of the leathery discs. "Look how he wiggles it."

"You better watch out—he might bite you!"

"Why would a pig bite someone who's feeding him?"

"You're not going to get me to touch it!"

Why wasn't Marvin interested in stroking a pig's snout? It didn't feel the way it looked—it felt soft and warm.

Dad turned his tractor into the driveway. "Let's go eat," Marvin said, as we tossed the rest of the beet tops into the pen.

After Grandpa and Grandma Johnson finished their last sips of coffee, she clumped her cane across the kitchen floor and up the stairway to their bedroom, where they had lived for nearly two years, since Marvin and I were six years old. Betty retreated into the bedroom we shared. Marvin sprawled across his bed with our stack of comic books. The *Farm Journal* sagged in Dad's lap as he nodded off in his easy chair in the living room.

I found Mom sitting on the step above the landing, halfway down the basement stairway, the skirt of her housedress draped between her legs. Three metal egg baskets sat on the landing beside a thirty-dozen egg crate.

"Can I help pack eggs?" I asked.

"If you want to. The dirty ones go in the bucket of soapy water. Be careful when you put them in. The cracked ones go in the coffee can."

After tucking one of the flat separators into the bottom of the crate, I unfolded a divider and spread it across the separator while Mom lifted an egg from the pail and rotated it in her hand.

"Make sure you put the pointed end down," she said, as she slid the egg into one of the thirty-six squares in the divider.

"Tell me about Marvin and me when we were small," I said, as I checked to see which end of the egg in my hand was more pointed. "About the things we did when we were little."

"Well, I've always said how good the two of you were. You entertained yourselves while I did my work."

"Tell me about the first time you let us go outside to play by ourselves—the time we took off across the field."

"Oh, that time." She placed another egg in a square. "You weren't very old, maybe two or three. When I went out to check up on you, you had disappeared. I looked everywhere. Finally, I saw the two of you halfway across Bengtson's muddy field. I had to send Winston after you with the car."

"Tell me how Marvin used to splash mud all over me."

"You liked to sit in the middle of the puddles," she said, dropping an egg into the can of cracked eggs. "He'd stand on the side and splash the water with a long stick. He stayed nice and clean, but you got covered with mud."

"What else did we do?"

"Let me think," she said, as she reached for another metal basket of eggs. "Marvin said lots of cute things. He used to call himself 'Munny,' and he called you 'Marin.' That was cute. It was cute, the way he liked to take his naps. Once, when it was naptime, I had to go looking for him. I finally found him, fast asleep, under his crib!"

She straightened the egg divider I had spread over the one we had just filled.

"He was always so good-natured. One of your dad's cousins watched you run ahead of him to grab a toy. 'What are you going to do about that?' she asked. 'He doesn't mind,' I said."

I didn't know I had grabbed toys before Marvin could get them. He may not have minded, but Mom's expression told me she didn't like that I had rushed ahead of him to snatch something he wanted.

"Did I do anything that was cute?"

"Oh yes, you were cute too. Once he had a cold and refused to take his cough medicine. You opened your mouth and swallowed it for him. He got better, so it must have worked."

"What else?"

"What more do you want me to tell?" she said, as she slid a dirty egg into the water.

CHAPTER 5

I had been unable to think of anything else as I counted down the months, the weeks, the days. I rearranged my pencil box, opened and closed the lid of my shiny new lunch pail. Mom sewed a cotton dress with short puffed sleeves and bought brown ankle-high, lace-up shoes for me. Marvin wore a striped, long-sleeved pullover shirt and a new pair of bib overalls.

When the day finally arrived, Mom drove our sister, Betty, and us two miles to Kandiyohi County School District No. 54. The one-room country school with white clapboard siding, twenty feet wide and twice as long, had a bell tower with a metal spire that pointed a stern finger high into the prairie sky. To Marvin and me, the school looked immense.

We followed Betty into the cloak hall. The smell of fresh varnish on the glistening wooden floor prickled the inside of my nostrils as we lined up our lunch pails on the shelf above the coat hooks. I stared at the columns of wooden desks bolted onto long, heavy planks. The seventh and eighth graders, some taller than Dad, sat in the biggest desks on the right, the middle grades in the two columns in the center, and the first graders in the smallest desks at the left. The windows, four on each of the two longer walls, had been scrubbed by our mothers, as had the blackboards that lined the spaces between them. A large oil burner stood in the right front corner of the room.

Grandpa Peterson and his five brothers and sisters and Grandma Peterson and her eleven brothers and sisters had walked to the first school, the one the settlers had built from logs. At that time, forty kids and one teacher squeezed into the single room. When Dad went to our school, built in 1900, there were still forty students. In 1947, two years after World War II had ended and the year Marvin and I started first grade, there were only twenty kids who attended the school.

We stood quietly beside our desks while Miss Noland, wearing a cotton dress and saddle shoes, led us in the Pledge of Allegiance. When she wound the clock on the wall, the ratcheting of the key echoed across the silent room.

Mom had worried that Marvin was too young to start school, but I had been so excited, she didn't feel right about holding me back. "How could I separate them," she said, "and send one to school without the other when they've always been together?" Marvin fell asleep, his head resting on his desk, at the time we had been taking our afternoon naps. He struggled to grip his pencil with his left hand, twisting his arm around the top of the paper to scratch out the ABCs. But Miss Noland was taken by his sparkly blue eyes, the tufts in his hair—the color of dandelion fluff—and his happy laugh.

"He's easy to love," she told Mom, reassuring her that Marvin was doing fine. "And Marilyn is smart."

I didn't fall asleep but was too embarrassed to raise my hand to ask permission to go to the outhouse. After wiggling and squirming and squeezing my legs together, I began to cry as a puddle spread across the floor beneath my desk. Miss Noland walked to the wooden telephone on the wall at the back of the room, and after cranking the handle several rounds, asked the operator to ring Mom on our party line.

"You don't need to ask permission to go to the outhouse," Miss Noland said after Mom brought me a dry dress. "Just raise your hand and I'll nod my head."

I raised my hand to ask permission to a scoop a blob of white paste from the big jar at the back of the room. When she nodded her head, I went to the outhouse instead.

Marvin's desk was never more than one or two desks away from mine. I felt more confident, more courageous, when he was nearby. But we never played together at school. On the very first day, I had become friends with Gayle Gjelhaug. I was lucky to have her in our grade as there were no girls in the three grades above us. Marvin found a friend, Darrell Steberg, also in our grade. He stood a head taller than Marvin but was too shy to say anything in school. We knew he lived with his mother and his grandparents because he didn't have a father. I tried to understand how that could be, because everyone except Jesus had a father.

Before we started school, I had never compared my twin to anyone else. But when I saw how fast David Smith—no bigger than Marvin—could run, I began to look at my brother in a different light. I felt disappointed in him when he had trouble tossing a basketball into the hoop behind the school or was unable to whack the softball as hard as the other boys his age. David could slam the ball over the heads of the fielders, and when Philip Gjerde—whose leg had been paralyzed during a polio epidemic the year before we started school—got a hit, David tore around the bases in his place. Marvin's hand-me-down glove had been made for someone who was right-handed, but I knew his glove was not the problem.

Until then, I had thought the world of my brother. I felt guilty for being disappointed in him, then ashamed of my selfish thoughts. When he looked dejected while waiting to be picked for a team, I wanted to shore him up, to make his happy smile return. At the same time, I was annoyed at him for not being good at sports, for not trying harder, for not being as fast as David Smith.

The Smith kids, with eyes as dark as their hair, didn't look like the rest of us, all Norwegians, except our family, who was Swedish. The Smiths went to the Unitarian church in Willmar. All the other kids were Lutherans, except our family, who went to the Salem Evangelical Mission Covenant Church. We thought Unitarians were one step away from being atheists. Some neighbors said the Smiths were communists, but we had no idea what that meant.

David scoured the shelves inside the Kandiyohi County bookmobile, a paneled van that came to our school four or five times a year, until he found a book he wanted to read. Not knowing how to look for a book, I grabbed two off the table and hurried out the door. The Smiths had books and an encyclopedia at home. Our family had *Little Black Sambo*, *Henny Penny*, and a few other books meant for little kids. Mom read the Bible and Dad read the *Farm Journal*. "Books are a waste of time," he said.

One day, I tossed a soft snowball into the boys' snow fort; David sneaked around the school to the fort Gayle and I had built and slammed me with a snowball packed into a ball of ice. Marvin had never smacked me like that. Once, during recess, I fought with David to claim first place when we lined up by the door; he punched me in the jaw so hard, I staggered. Marvin had never hit me. He never protested if I went first. After that, I stayed away from David.

The night I stayed at Gayle's house, her four brothers showed me how they could drink Kool-Aid by sucking it up their noses. They milked their cows by hand before they went to school in the morning and again before they ate their evening meal. I was happy we had two milking machines so Marvin didn't have to get up early to help Dad.

When the teacher assigned our weekly duties, Marvin worked with Darrell and I worked with Gayle. She and I stood on opposite sides of the pump handle when we got water duty, pumping as hard as we could to pull the icy water up from the deep well. It spilled on my shoes as we dragged the pail up the steps and into the schoolhouse and splashed on our dresses as we poured the water into the big water crock. We filled the washbasin, even though no one ever washed their hands—unless they got coated with paste when working in our *Alice and Jerry* workbooks or smeared with plaster of Paris while filling the molds of George Washington and Abraham Lincoln. Farm kids didn't worry about dirt. Marvin wiped his hands on his overalls, and I wiped mine on my dress.

When Gayle and I got bell duty, the rope lifted us off the floor. Some of the older boys yanked the rope so hard, the bell flipped over in the tower. "It was an accident!" they said, but I knew they were lying.

Gayle and I never got flag duty. Only boys were allowed to raise the flag.

The fall before Betty turned thirteen and Marvin and I turned nine, the farmers, after much contention, had decided to send the seventh and eighth grades to the town school. When Betty was partway through seventh grade, she turned to Mom:

"You need a new girdle."
"My old girdle is doing just fine."

A few weeks later, Betty slammed the door when she came home and dumped her books on the table. "Why didn't you tell me you were P.G.," she fumed, "instead of me having to find out about it in school!"

I knew "P.G." meant pregnant. But neither Marvin nor I knew, nor had Betty known, that Mom was pregnant. She hadn't told us, with her due date just three months away.

During those three months, the flat prairie land was deluged with snow. Our school closed for two weeks while snowplows were brought in from the surrounding regions to help break through the massive pileup of drifts that blocked the country roads.

Marvin and I liked being "snowed in" at home with no means to go anywhere. Mom heated up the vegetables she had canned, boiled potatoes we stored in a bin in our basement, and fried meat she kept frozen in packages on the porch above our entry. We drank milk from our cows and ate eggs from our hens. Because the creamery truck was unable to pick up our cream cans, Dad made slop for the pigs by mixing it with their feed. When he finished his chores, he shoveled out tunnels for us in the drifts next to the windmill. "You look like a polar bear!" Marvin said, as we burrowed through the holes. Dad started up his tractor with his snow scoop and piled up a mound at the top of the hill in the pasture, giving us a fast start on our wooden skies and runner sleds. He wrapped his legs around us on the toboggan as we whizzed down the hill. After supper, Mom popped popcorn, drenching it with butter, while we played Chinese checkers with Dad. He feathered the old maid cards in his hand and smiled as he slid one card higher than the others.

"Dad, is that the old maid?" I asked. "Are you trying to trick us?"

Winter did not release its hold on the prairie land until April, initiating a runoff from the enormous amount of melting snow that turned the gravel roads into an impassable slurry. Dad hitched up the two-wheeled trailer to his tractor and used it to drive Marvin and me to school. "You have polka dots all over your face," Marvin said, pointing at the splatters of mud on my cheeks as we sat down in our desks. I didn't mind the polka dots—riding in the trailer was fun.

In mid-April, I spent the day watching the hands on the big clock hanging on the wall mete out the seconds while I waited for Dad to arrive at our school to pick up Marvin and me. It was the day he was to bring Mom and our baby brother, Mark, home from the hospital.

I raced through the kitchen and into Mom and Dad's bedroom where I stared at the little baby's pink face as he lay in a wicker basket. Mom could not withstand my pleading. She sat me in the middle of the bed, picked up the sleeping baby, and placed him in my arms.

Marvin stood at the side of the room and watched me as I examined our brother's tiny fingers, stroked the soft skin on his little bald head. But a baby brother did not enchant a nine-year-old boy in the same way he enchanted a nine-year-old girl, who cradled him in her lap while she fed him his bottles, cooed at him until he smiled, rocked him until he fell asleep. A baby boy did not enthrall a nine-year-old brother the way he enthralled a thirteen-year-old sister, distracting her from her new world of friends in the town school. A baby did not captivate an older brother the way he captivated Mom and Dad, who were overjoyed with their new son.

Mark had turned two by the time Marvin—his eyes now obscured behind black framed glasses—and I started sixth grade, our last year in the country school. I felt proud when Mrs. Johnson, our teacher that year, asked me to help the younger kids. I squeezed into their small desks to assist them as they worked in their reading workbooks and to hold up arithmetic flashcards for them in the back of the room.

Even so, I felt jealous when Mom said, "Those Smith kids are so smart, they always end up at the top of their class!" I sped down the long columns of four-digit numbers when Mrs. Johnson lined the sixth graders up at the blackboards for races in arithmetic. I was determined to beat David Smith—and sometimes I did.

Marvin didn't care who won the races. He wasn't fast at arithmetic.

When Mrs. Johnson handed out the roles in the plays for our Christmas program, Marvin didn't want a long part; he wanted fewer lines to memorize. When David asked me how many lines I got, I said, "Just as many as you!"

Two weeks before our program, Dad and several other fathers built a stage from cinderblocks and wooden planks. I helped thread the blue calico curtains onto the baling-wire lines.

Mrs. Johnson shushed the little kids, jumping up and down as they peeked between the curtains while their mothers and fathers found places on the planks held up by the seats of our desks. The first graders shivered with fright as they stood on the stage and stumbled through their pieces. In loud whispers, the older kids prompted those in the plays when they forgot their lines. Everyone wanted to pull the calico curtains.

We ended our program the way we always did, with a Christmas pageant. The younger girls, dressed as angels, stood guard while holding up the wings our mothers had sewn from worn-out sheets. Darrell and Philip, wearing bathrobes as their costumes, offered gold, frankincense, and myrrh, made from tinfoil and colored paper. Marvin wore a gunny sack he found in our granary as he kneeled alongside the other shepherds. David, playing the part of Joseph, stood beside Gayle, who held a doll wrapped in a blue blanket, while I recited the Christmas story from the Gospel of Luke:

> And Joseph also went up from Galilee, out of the city
> of Nazareth, into Judea, unto the city of David, which
> is called Bethlehem... (Luke 2:4)

When everyone stopped clapping, the men on the school board handed out brown paper bags filled with candy to each of the children and Red Delicious apples wrapped in red tissue paper to everyone.

Marvin and I squeezed into the back seat of our 1950 Ford as Dad chipped the ice off the windshield.

"Do you have any chocolate-covered mints?" I asked, as we rustled through our paper bags. "I'll trade you for my chocolate-covered cherries."

I knew the cherries were his favorite candy. He knew I loved the mints.

The rays of the May sun warmed my face as Gayle and I swiveled in lazy circles on the swings, lunch pails balanced on our laps. "I wonder what it's going to be like, going to the town school," I said. "Do you know how many kids there are in Betty's grade? Twenty-seven!"

"I hope it doesn't happen to us like it does to some of the kids," she said. "They find new friends, and then they aren't friends anymore."

Gayle had been the only girl my age in our one-room school. I wanted to be part of a group of girls, to invite them to our house for slumber parties, like my sister did, when they pranced around in their bras and panties while talking about the boys they liked and the teachers they hated. I wanted to grow breasts, to have periods, to find out about sex. When I asked Betty what the box of sanitary napkins that suddenly appeared on our closet shelf was for, she said Mom had only muttered a couple of words before hurrying out of the room. Mom never mentioned anything about sex to me—not then, not ever.

The afternoon Tom Cat had clamped his teeth on the back of Mama Cat's neck, Mom had dropped her trowel, rushed into the house to grab her broom, and whacked the cats until they ran off in opposite directions.

"I hate it when they fight like that!" she said, as she returned to weeding her marigolds.

"Why is she so mad at the cats?" I asked Marvin after she finished her gardening.

"Maybe she thinks they'll get hurt."

"Why were they fighting?"

"How should I know?" he said, looking as puzzled as I felt.

I never mentioned anything to Marvin about breasts or periods. We most certainly did not talk about sex.

After our baby brother was born, I spent my time learning how to jiggle safety pins through his cloth diapers before pulling on his rubber pants. I got down on my hands and knees and slid his arms and legs back and forth to teach him how to crawl and then set up a line of chairs to entice him to risk a few steps to get from one chair to the next. When he refused to take a nap, I pulled him in the red Radio Flyer wagon in our driveway until he fell asleep.

Marvin spent his time building bird houses with the toolset Mom and Dad had bought for him. He lay next to his bike and attached Rook cards to the frame to make a motor sound as they slapped against the spokes. In school, he played with Darrell, and I played with Gayle. At church, we no longer sat between Mom and Dad; he scrunched down in a pew with the other boys our age, and I wriggled in with the girls in the pew in front of the boys.

A crack had opened in the bonds that cemented us together. When I saw him standing alone, I felt as if I belonged beside him, but another part of me wanted to break away and go off with my friends.

I felt as if we were being torn apart.

During one of our last weeks in the one-room school, I chucked the crusts of my bologna sandwich into my lunch pail and pivoted my swing to face Gayle.

"I have an idea," I said. "Let's make a secret club."

"What kind of secret club?"

"A club where we tell everything we know about babies, and how people 'do it' to get a baby started."

Sharon Henjum and Betty Hauge, a couple of grades below Gayle and me, agreed to meet us in the girls' outhouse. Gayle pushed the warped door shut so I could jam the hook all the way into the metal eye. Sharon sat on one end of the dank bench with Gayle on the other end and Betty in the space between the two holes.

I squinted in the dim light filtering in through the opening near the peak of the roof and cleared my throat twice, like Dad did before he gave an important speech.

"I'll give the first report for our secret club," I said. "The name of my report is 'Maternity Tops.'" I told them that the tops had to be sewed with lots of gathers in the front so the material would hide the mother's stomach where the baby was growing and that some mothers, like mine, just wore bigger housedresses when their bellies got really fat. My report seemed too short, so I elaborated—"Maternity tops can be made from different materials like corduroy or seersucker. The material can be different colors, like red or blue or green." At that point, I had exhausted what I knew about the topic.

All three girls were staring at the floor. I turned to Betty Hauge, thinking her mother might have told her something about sex.

"It's your turn to give a report at the next meeting."

Her cheeks flushed with blotches of red, but she was too shy to say "no" to a sixth-grade girl.

Our dog, Daisy, sprang from my side and erupted in a fit of barking as a car turned into our driveway. I grabbed her collar as Mrs. Gjelhaug, her hair wrapped in a white scarf, stepped out of the car.

"She won't bite you," I said, "she always barks like that."

"She sure does make a fuss, doesn't she?" Mrs. Gjelhaug smiled. "Is your mother home?"

"Tell her to come on in," Mom said, untying her apron and combing her fingers through her hair.

I pulled a chair up to the kitchen table across from Mrs. Gjelhaug as they chatted about the best time to put their tomatoes in so they wouldn't be nipped by the frost, when the ground would be dry enough for the men to get out in the fields, and the height of the new silo the Husebys had put up. Mrs. Gjelhaug turned to Mom and tipped her head towards me.

"Marilyn, why don't you go out and play for a while," Mom said.

I found Daisy sleeping under a honeysuckle bush by the windmill. She growled as I worked a wad of cockleburs out from behind her ear and snapped at my hand as I untangled a lump of fur knotted up under her collar.

After what seemed like hours, Mrs. Gjelhaug walked out onto the porch. She smiled before opening the door to her car and waved as she turned out of our driveway.

"What did Mrs. Gjelhaug want?" I asked, rushing into the kitchen.

Mom opened the refrigerator door and jammed the cream pitcher onto a shelf.

"She said you started a club in school that's *not very nice.*" She slammed the refrigerator door shut and glared at me. "There'll be *no more* clubs like that!"

I was stunned that Mrs. Gjelhaug knew about our club, stunned by the rage that flushed Mom's neck.

The deadbolt clunked as I rotated the key in the lock. The coils in the spring pressed down on my chest as I squeezed under the bed. Why would someone tattle on her best friend? Marvin and I never told on each other, no matter what we did. If Gayle didn't want to be in a secret club, she could have said something to me instead of telling her mother.

Maybe it wasn't Gayle. Maybe it was Betty Hauge. Maybe Betty wanted to get out of giving the next report. Their farm wasn't far from Gjelhaugs' place. Her mother could have gone to have a talk with Mrs. Gjelhaug.

It could have been Sharon Henjum. They were renters and lived on the farm next to the Gjelhaugs'.

I still trusted Marvin, but we had branched off onto separate paths. My shirt tangled into the coils of the spring as I pushed further under the bed while breathing in the hot dampness of my own breath.

I felt alone. Everything was changing.

CHAPTER 6

I knew the Bible was God's Word and tried to make sense of the readings, but I was hungry and wanted to eat. Marvin was staring at his empty plate. He hated having to wait for breakfast. Even so, we sat quietly while Dad read a chapter and said a prayer. But after a few weeks, Dad found it too hard to come in from the morning milking in time to finish family devotions before Betty had to catch the bus. Mom tried placing the Bible on his plate before supper, but after working all day in the fields, he was too famished to lead us in devotions. She was disappointed to not be able to find a time that worked. I knew I should also be disappointed, but secretly, I was relieved.

Mom read the Bible every day, starting with the book of Genesis, and when she finished the book of Revelation, she went back to the beginning. She made certain we followed the commandment "Thou shalt not take the name of the Lord thy God in vain" by prohibiting us from saying "darn it" or "dang it" as substitutes for "damn it"—a strictly forbidden phrase. We were not allowed to say "what the heck" in place of the blasphemous words "what in the hell" or "oh gosh" in place of "oh my God"—a phrase considered sacrilegious. I clamped my lips together to prevent the sinful words from popping out whenever the devil tried to sneak them into my mouth.

She kept our minds pure by warning us about playing with the forbidden parts of our bodies. "Why does Mom say we shouldn't play with our bellybuttons?" I had asked Marvin when we were still taking our Saturday baths together, careful to keep my fingers from sliding toward the forbidden knot of tissue in the middle of my belly.

"I don't know. Maybe because it might turn inside out."

Pastor Wickman warned us to beware the sins of the flesh that could prevent us from entering the Kingdom of Heaven. I found the list—adultery, fornication, uncleanness, lasciviousness, idolatry, witchcraft, hatred, variance, emulations, wrath, strife, seditions, heresies, envyings, murders, drunkenness, and revellings—in the book of Galatians. I had no idea what most of these words meant.

Mom did not have to worry about Marvin and me succumbing to worldly pleasures because we were too young to go out into the world. She worried about Betty, who begged to go to the Willmar Theater with her friends. But Pastor Wickman said that movies showed people doing sinful things, movie stars led sinful lives, and movies made worldly pleasures look like fun. When Betty went on a date, Mom warned her, "Nothing good happens after midnight!" and watched the clock until she returned. I promised myself I would always come in early when I dated so she would never have to worry about me.

Marvin didn't pay any attention to Mom's worries about Betty nor did he pay any attention to Pastor Wickman's sermons. He waited for the services to end so he could hang out with the boys in the parking lot beside the church.

When Mrs. Wickman told the junior choir to "sing with joy," I sang as loudly as I could. I was thrilled when she asked me to sing a solo verse and was jealous if she asked someone else. Marvin had a good singing voice, but he slouched down in the back row with the other boys.

When Mrs. Wickman asked the junior youth group to memorize the story about Nicodemus, when he asked Jesus how a man could be born again when he is old—"[C]an he enter the second time into his mother's womb, and be born?"—I sat cross-legged on my bed, Bible in my lap, and memorized all twenty-one verses of the chapter. Mrs. Wickman smiled as I recited them:

> Jesus answered, Verily, verily, I say unto thee, Except
> a man be born of water and of the Spirit, he cannot
> enter into the kingdom of God.

That which is born of the flesh is flesh; and that which is born of the Spirit is spirit.

Marvel not that I said unto thee, Ye must be born again. (John 3: 5–7)

I wanted Mrs. Wickman to put her hand on my shoulder and make me feel warm all over by giving me a hug. I wanted her to love me as much as I loved her.

Marvin didn't care what Mrs. Wickman thought of him. He wanted the meetings to end so he could watch the older boys show off for the popular girls and listen to them brag about how many seconds it took for their cars to go from zero to sixty.

When Pastor Wickman leaned his lanky frame over the wooden pulpit—electric organ on his left, grand piano on his right—in the unadorned sanctuary, there wasn't an empty space in the pews. Families with small children and mothers holding babies sat near the back, teenaged boys filed into the pews on the side, and teenaged girls crowded into the pews in front of the boys.

Pastor Wickman preached straight from the Bible. He didn't need to use notes because he was led by the Holy Spirit. I knew the devil was tempting me when I longed for Pastor Wickman to put his arms around me. But when he pleaded with the sinners, telling them that they would spend eternity in the fires of hell if they weren't saved by being "born again," I shivered in the pew.

As I lay on the long, cool grass at the end of our lawn, waiting for the trace of a breeze, I tried to imagine what it would be like to live forever in time without end. If Jesus returned to lift up those who had been saved when Marvin and I were still twelve years old, would we always be Mom and Dad's children in heaven? Would Grandpa Johnson, who had died a year earlier, always have a Swedish brogue? Would my cousin's twin, who had only lived six weeks, have to live forever as a tiny baby?

On the airless July nights, I sprawled across Betty's and my bed, wiping the sweat from my forehead as I worried about devils and the flames of hell while trying to fall asleep. Before the roosters crowed in a new day, I woke from nightmares about sinners burning in time without end.

I realized I was a sinner. I needed to be saved.

The pews were packed when Marvin squeezed in with the boys, and I with the girls, to hear the visiting evangelist who had come to hold revival services in our church. I glanced at the faces in the crowded sanctuary as we sang the opening hymn, felt their eager expectation that the Holy Spirit would move through the congregation and bring an awakening to the people.

I looked at Mom, her head bowed in prayer, and at Dad, holding my brother Mark in his lap, as the evangelist held up his Bible and warned the sinners. I crunched down between my friends and wiped my damp palms on the skirt of my dress as I pictured flames curling around my face, devils laughing as I screamed, no hope of escaping from time that lasts forever.

The hymnal trembled in my hands as we sang the first verse of the altar call hymn:

> Just as I am, without one plea
> But that Thy blood was shed for me
> And that Thou bidd'st me come to Thee
> O Lamb of God, I come! I come!

My heart beat hard as Pastor Wickman pleaded with the sinners, the organ vibrating, the evangelist praying, as we waited for the awakening, for the stirring of the Spirit, for the Spirit to move among the sinners.

"If you feel the Spirit speaking to you," Pastor Wickman said, his voice sounding warm and welcoming, "come and kneel at the front of the church and confess your sins. He will forgive you and make you whole."

The Holy Spirit was speaking to me, but I did not want to walk down the aisle past the pew where my cousins Marian Holmgren and Arlou Halvorson, who had already been saved, bowed their heads in prayer; past my cousins, Sheldon Johnson and Harry Johnson, hunched down with their friends, waiting for the service to end; past my sister, sneaking glances at the other girls even though Pastor Wickman had said, "with all eyes closed"; past Marvin, who felt no need to be saved and was cemented to the pew with the boys our age, the ones who poked each other and snickered during the Sunday morning sermons; past the deacons, who turned and glared at me when I passed notes to my friends.

I clutched the hymnal to steady my hands as Pastor Wickman asked us to sing the second verse:

> Just as I am, tho' tossed about
> With many a conflict, many a doubt
> Fightings and fears within, without
> O Lamb of God, I come! I come!

I had fightings within, fightings without. Even though I knew it was a sin, I sneaked oatmeal raisin cookies from the big, apple-shaped cookie jar when Mom was in the henhouse picking eggs. I spied on Betty through the keyhole in the bathroom door while she got ready for a date. I took the half with the most almonds when Marvin and I divided a Hershey bar. Instead of tithing the spending money Mom gave us and giving it to our missionaries in Japan and Africa and rural Wisconsin, I spent it on Tootsie Rolls and Turkish Taffy.

I wanted the Holy Spirit to cleanse me of my sins, but my legs were glued to the pew. "Dear Jesus, give me the strength to walk down the aisle," I silently prayed, my chin pressed against my chest as I waited for the awakening, for the Holy Spirit to move among the people.

As if in a whirlwind, the Spirit grabbed hold of me, lifted me to my feet, and transported me down the aisle to the front of the church, where I crumpled onto my knees in front of Pastor Wickman.

No one spoke as Dad drove home from the service. He lifted Mark from Mom's lap and carried him to his crib in their downstairs bedroom. Betty and Marvin hurried up the stairway.

"I'll pray every day that Jesus will keep you strong," Mom said, placing her hand on my shoulder.

CHAPTER 7

If Betty had leaned any closer to our vanity mirror, her nose would have bumped into the glass. A pimple wasn't the worst thing in the world, I thought, sitting cross-legged on my side of our bed as she pressed two fingernails against a little bump amidst a splash of freckles. She tipped her head over her knees and counted two hundred strokes while pulling a brush through her honey-blond hair. After puckering her lips around a couple of bobby pins, she sectioned off a square of hair with her long black comb and stretched the clump above her head.

"You'll never believe it—it was so much fun!" I said, as she dunked the comb into a glass of water. "As soon as we got into the gym, I met a girl named Connie. We laughed so hard! I can't remember her last name, something starting with R, I think. She has a sister in your grade named Betty. Isn't that funny? Just like me—a sister named Betty!"

"Ronholdt," Betty mumbled, the bobby pins bouncing between her pursed lips. "Betty Ronholdt."

"That's it. Ronholdt. Anyhow, Connie and I started giggling. We couldn't stop. Mr. Gulsvig was handing out the schedule for the seventh graders. There's more than fifty of us, can you believe it? We had no idea what we were doing. Everyone went running up and down the halls—I about crashed into a bunch of boys—and then we couldn't find our lockers!"

Betty pried a bobby pin open against her front tooth and slid it across the curl she had wound around her index finger. She pulled another bobby pin from between her lips, wedged it open, and shoved it across the first.

"Mom says you shouldn't open bobby pins like that because you might chip the enamel on your tooth."

She rotated the brass handle of the hand mirror until she could see a reflection of the back of her head in the vanity mirror. After giving each pin curl a quick pat, she parted off another square of hair and started a second row of curls.

"Anyhow, when we were done with math, all the country kids ran down to the gym for hot lunch. The cooks plopped mashed potatoes on our plates—I couldn't believe it; they used an ice cream scoop! Connie and I sat down with her friend Jean, she has a really funny last name, and Diane Beckman. She has a sister in your grade too. Two friends with sisters in your grade! Isn't that funny? Then a bunch of boys sat down at the table next to ours. They pointed at the rice pudding—'Oh, look, maggots!' they said—we about died laughing. Then a teacher came over and said, 'All right, it's time to settle down.'"

Betty spread a spiderweb hairnet across her fingertips and pulled it over her hair, picking it free as it stuck to the bobby pins. After lifting a blue jar of Noxzema from her top vanity drawer, she rubbed shiny blobs in circles on her forehead and cheeks. She clicked off the vanity lamps and turned to me.

"Well, the office called me out of class," she said. "One of the teachers found Marvin crying in the hall."

My throat seized up. I couldn't swallow. I slid under our blanket and pulled it over my head.

"It's not your fault he got lost," Betty said as she slid into her side of our bed. "It's time for him to figure out how to take care of himself—just because he's your twin doesn't mean you always have to watch out for him!"

I pushed my face into my pillow to choke back my sobs, so Betty wouldn't know I was crying. She was kind and generous to me, but I knew she thought Marvin was odd. She didn't understand that, even though we were apart, I could see how he had wrinkled his forehead, the way his eyes had glistened with pain as he watched the kids vanish into the rooms, leaving him standing there, alone, in an empty hallway, with no one to watch out for him.

He had never gotten lost in the one-room school. I always knew where he was while he and I pedaled our bicycles over the two miles of gravel roads to the school, and after we got there, even though he played with Darrell and I with Gayle. But when we stepped into the bus to the town school, I slid into a seat near the front, and he strode past me to a seat with the boys in the back. He passed me on the way to his locker, halfway down the long hallway of the three-story school. Instead of six kids in our grade, we had fifty-two, with hundreds of kids in seventh through twelfth grade. There were dozens of town kids we'd never met and busloads of country kids we didn't know, kids from farms more than fifteen miles away, spilling through the corridors, dashing from classroom to classroom.

I had forgotten to watch out for my brother, to make sure he found his way. He got lost because he was used to following me.

Sometimes I felt lost. The town girls wore blouses tucked into flared skirts, not dresses with puffy sleeves and gathers at the waist like the hand-me-downs I wore. Their hair didn't hang down like stalks of straw, a clump of crooked bangs flopping above their eyes. I asked Betty to teach me how to set my hair in pin curls, but my stubborn hair sproinged out of the bobby pins while I slept. In the morning, my curls had corners.

The town girls sometimes snickered when I talked.

"Marilyn, say 'Christmas,'" Jean Baker said, as we sat on the bleachers in the gymnasium, waiting for a pep rally to begin.

"Why?" I asked.

"I like to hear the way you say your Ss."

"What's wrong with the way I say them?"

"Nothing's wrong with them. I just like the way they make a kind of a hissing sound."

I shut the door to Betty's and my bedroom and practiced saying "Christmas" until I no longer could detect any hissing in my voice.

"Does this sound better?" I asked Jean.

"Now your Ss make a buzzing sound. Sort of the way a Z sounds."

Even so, I had my chance to beat the town kids when Mrs. Adams sent the seventh graders to the blackboards for races in arithmetic. And when she had us race against the eighth graders, I beat them too.

Mom didn't say anything when I won the arithmetic races, but when Marvin won a spelling bee, she went on and on about it while we were eating supper, bragged to Grandpa and Grandma Peterson, and brought it up when our aunts and uncles visited us. I knew jealousy was a sin, so I prayed to Jesus, asking Him to forgive me.

By the end of seventh grade, I had grown a half head taller than Marvin. Until then, we had always been the same size. Mom made an appointment with Dr. Helvig, the Kerkhoven doctor, as she worried that he had stopped growing. After examining him, the doctor said, "Be patient. Boys start their adolescent growth spurt later than girls." Mom hadn't noticed he was just as tall as most of the boys in our grade, only that he looked small next to me.

He began to make strange coughing sounds, as if something had caught in the back of his throat, when we sat down for our meals.

"Mom, tell Marvin to stop making those weird noises," Betty said.

He shoved his fork back and forth beside his plate and skidded his glass of milk from side to side when he talked.

"Stop moving your glass around," Mom said. "You'll spill your milk."

"It's not because I'm moving the glass. It's because these glasses are too tippy," he said as he toppled the glass, splashing milk across the table.

Mom drove to Willmar and bought water glasses with thick, heavy bottoms. He knocked those over too.

He began to shrug his right shoulder, as if trying to brush a mosquito away from his ear.

"Stop doing that with your shoulder," Mom said. "You're going to form a habit."

"It's because I have a kink in my neck. I'm trying to loosen it up."

I felt sorry for my brother, but at the same time was embarrassed by the way he hunched his shoulder and made strange sounds in front of my friends.

"Why is he getting so many bad habits?" I asked Mom.

"He'll outgrow them," she said.

But the twin who had laughed with me as we ran down the long rows of corn could not stop his tics and shrugs. I watched him standing at the edge of the group of popular boys in our grade as they joked and laughed, the way he hurried to keep up with them as they made their way down the corridor.

At the same time, I was trying to fit in with the popular girls, listening to the way they talked and wanting to wear skirts and blouses that looked like the ones they wore.

Part of me wanted to help my twin. But another part of me wanted to be free from watching out for him.

CHAPTER 8

An Arctic front raged through the prairie land, rattling the windows in my bedroom as I rotated the hand mirror so I could see the back of my head. My ponytail was askew. I tugged the rubber band until I had centered the clump of my thick, blond, stick-straight hair. Betty's eyebrow pencil lay in the top drawer where she had dropped it when she went to Minneapolis to take a secretarial program at the Minnesota School of Business. But I had given up penciling my colorless eyebrows. The high bridge on my prominent nose, inherited from Dad, made it impossible for me to look like Grace Kelly.

After coating my lips with bright pink lipstick, I stepped back from the mirror for a final once-over—black angora pullover topped with a white detachable collar; straight woolen skirt ending halfway down my calves; bobby socks, folded down twice; penny loafers, but no pennies. The town girls never put pennies in their loafers.

I stacked my McCall's sewing pattern for home economics on top of my ninth-grade algebra book and headed for the stairway but stopped at the doorway to Marvin's room. He was standing in front of his mirror while pulling a comb through his greased hair, a track of parallel lines streaming from his forehead to the back of his head. None of the town kids slicked their hair back like that. He had put on his favorite Orlon shirt with a gradation of colors—black at his hips, gray at his belly, white at his chest—the same shirt he always wore.

"Why don't you wear one of your new shirts?" I asked.

"What's wrong with this shirt?"

"Look at it." I pointed at his belly. "It's old. It's pilled. It's covered with little black knots because you wear it practically every day!"

"That's not because it's old," he said, smoothing his fingers over the knots. "It's supposed to look that way—it's the kind of material it's made from."

"If it's supposed to look that way, why does it only have knots in the front?" I walked into his closet and pulled two hangers from the rod. "Why don't you wear one of these that I bought for you? They look really nice." I had given him the shirts three months earlier, for our fifteenth birthday, after buying them at the J. C. Penney store on a shopping trip to Willmar with Mom. One was a gray-and-blue plaid; the other had rust-and-gold vertical stripes. He had yet to wear either one.

I dangled the hangers in front of his face. "These are the kind of shirts the other kids are wearing."

"There's nothing wrong with this shirt," he said, picking at one of the little black knots on his belly. "The bumps are part of the pattern."

"You know how the kids make fun of John Moon because he always wears flannel shirts? Well, they'll make fun of you too if you keep wearing that same old shirt!"

At times, the popular kids did make fun of him, but I would never hurt him by telling him that. He blinked hard if someone teased him; I could see his distress flash through his eyes. The boys watched what they said when I was around, but sometimes they forgot he was my twin.

"This is *not* a flannel shirt," Marvin said, scowling at me. "I *like* this shirt."

"I didn't say it was a flannel shirt—I said it was a worn-out, pilled shirt. Besides, no one wears short-sleeved shirts in the middle of winter—it's freezing out!"

"This shirt is *not* worn out."

"Fine." I flung the two new shirts onto his bed. "Why don't you wear it every day?"

At least he had gotten out of bed.

A year earlier, after waking him for the third time, Mom had planted herself in his doorway. "From now on I'm *not* waking you," she said. "You get yourself out of bed. If you miss the bus, I'm *not* going to drive you to school. And I'm *not* writing any excuses!"

After missing the bus a couple of times, he cobbled together two windup alarm clocks in a pie tin and set them on a stool next to the head of his bed. No one could sleep through that racket.

The clanging was even worse than the grating alarm that spewed out from a buzzer attached to a metallic pad placed under his bottom sheet, an apparatus Mom had borrowed from Mrs. Gjelhaug. She had decided to intervene when Dad became increasingly upset with Marvin, who wet the bed despite Dad waking him and walking him to the bathroom every night. The relentless sound reverberated through our bedrooms whenever his sheet got wet, continuing until it woke him, along with Betty and me.

After a couple of months, he began to wake up before the alarm went off. It took Dad a lot longer to simmer down.

I understood Dad's frustration, but I felt sorry for my brother. It was as if the buzzer dredged him up from some subterranean place—somewhere so deep it prevented him from wakening during the night to go to the bathroom, from wakening in the morning to get up for school, or wakening in the afternoon to help Dad with his work.

Marvin had never mentioned the bedwetting. Neither had I.

I reached for the sugar bowl when I heard him clomping down the stairway. He screeched his chair up to the table and skidded his glass of milk from side to side.

"There's nothing wrong with this shirt," he said, directing the anger in his eyes at me.

"You're right," I said. "It's a *fine* shirt."

Once he got stuck on a topic, he would not let it go. He talked about it, obsessed over it, even after the conversation had long since moved on to something else.

I glanced at Mom. If she got involved, she'd side with him.

"I *love* that shirt," I said. "Now eat your cereal. I'm sick of Clinton getting mad because he has to hold the bus for you."

He fixed his elbows on the table and leaned over his bowl, scooping the cereal into his mouth. Mom had given up telling him to mind his manners.

He never listened to her. He never listened to any of us.

A month earlier Marvin had become furious when Mom told him it was time to change his clothes because our guests, two of her sisters and their families, were about to arrive for a dinner party. I had already put all five leaves in our dining room table and set it for sixteen people.

"No one ever tells me anything," he said.

"How could you have missed it?" I had said as he fumed. "We were eating supper. You were sitting right there in your chair. We must have spent at least ten minutes talking about it."

After gobbling down half his cereal, he launched another diatribe at me. "Mom bought this shirt for me, and I like it."

I wanted to dump his cereal over his head. The only way to get him to drop a topic was to walk away. Even then, he'd pick up where he had left off the minute I returned.

I shoved my chair away from the table and grabbed my car coat from the entryway. The frigid air sliced into my lungs as I stepped out onto the porch. I checked the thermometer Dad had bolted to the side of the house—sixteen degrees below zero. I yanked the hood of my coat over my forehead and braced myself against the wind. Spirals of snow curled around my legs as I trudged between the banks of snow piled up along the sides of the driveway. I ducked into the shelter, not much bigger than a telephone booth, that Dad had built from corrugated steel to protect us from the wind. My breath flew off in frozen clouds as I watched for the yellow eyes of the bus.

The snow squeaked and crunched as Clinton pumped the brakes. I stepped out of the shelter and saw Marvin leaning into the wind as he ran down the driveway.

"He's right behind me," I said, my breath hanging in a haze as I brushed past Clinton.

He frowned, adjusting his conductor's cap before bracing his elbows on the steering wheel. I hunched down in my usual seat partway down the aisle. A gust of frigid air trailed Marvin as he trudged to the back of the bus where the older boys sat.

Half a mile down the gravel road going south, Clinton stopped and waited for Charlie Bengtson. He never muttered when he had to wait for Charlie, just honked the horn a couple of times and worked his wad of gum while propping his arms on the steering wheel.

Charlie had repeated the first and second grades before passing into third grade; although he spoke both Norwegian and Swedish, he had yet to learn English. At times, when he refused to go to school, we could hear his mother yelling at him in Norwegian.

A couple of summers earlier, Marvin and I had seen Charlie fishing in the small lake next to their place. We had been following the creek that snaked through the Bengtsons' pasture. I was afraid of them and their strange ways, but Marvin had wanted to see what Charlie was doing.

"What're you fishing?" Marvin said, after we hopped around the deep holes the cows had trampled in the mud.

"Bullheads," Charlie said, glancing our way.

"You're using worms for bait?" Marvin asked, as Charlie threaded his hook through a clump of angleworms, their ends wriggling in all directions.

"Yup. You gotta pile 'em on."

"You're using old sparkplugs for weights?" Marvin said, moving two steps closer.

"Yup. You gotta sink the hook into the mud. They swim right on the bottom."

He swung his line in a wide arc, the sparkplugs splashing into the water twenty feet out from the shore.

"Skin 'em and fry 'em in butter. They're real tasty."

Marvin and I stared at the bullheads, the color of mud with beady eyes and sharp feelers poking out of their flat heads, as Charlie reeled one after another up the bank. We had not known there were bull-heads in the lake. Nor had we imagined people would eat such an ugly fish.

I forgot about the bullheads as I scraped a space in the bus's frosted window and saw Charlie zigzagging his way around the snowdrifts. There were no poles to guide him down their long driveway because they did not have a telephone, nor did they have electricity.

A blast of icy air escorted him into the bus. His straw-colored hair straggled across his flushed cheeks as he slid into an empty seat, his black-domed lunch bucket—the kind the farmers brought to the field—balanced in his lap.

Clinton didn't have to honk at the next stop, a half mile farther down the road. Our double cousins—Dad's sister had married Mom's brother—were always waiting beside their mailbox.

During the summers, we had ridden our bikes back and forth from their farm to ours. Margaret and I built playhouses in the woods and molded dishes from the clods of clay we dug up next to our wind-mill, while Marvin and Jerry careened down the steep slope next to the retirement-farm barn in our red Radio Flyer wagon. They joined us to play tag in the pigweed that towered over our heads behind our henhouse.

Once, we had hidden in a cornfield and played doctor.

Clinton jolted me out of my daydreams when he started pumping the brakes as we approached the next crossroad. He brought the bus to a standstill.

"Now what's wrong?" Marvin shouted over the boys, who were making a ruckus in the back of the bus.

Clinton clamped the buckles on his four-buckle overshoes and trudged up to a drift that blocked the road. He tested it with a series of kicks.

"Maybe you need to put some chains on this thing," Marvin shouted as Clinton slid back into the driver's seat.

"Come on, Clinton! You can do it!" we all shouted while he shifted the bus into reverse.

A year earlier, the bus had gotten stuck in the middle of a snow-drift. By the time we had walked to the nearest farmhouse, our noses were white from the cold. The farmer pulled on his parka and plugged in the block heater on his tractor while his wife cooked a large kettle of cocoa with milk from their morning's milking.

The cocoa felt warm in my stomach, making me think of the cocoa Mom had made for Marvin and me while Dad shoveled a clearing on a slough, tied on his hockey skates, and circled the ice with us.

"You have a white mustache," Marvin had said, laughing while we slurped the frothy marshmallows from our steaming cups.

Clinton had put more than thirty feet of open road between the bus and the snowdrift. He shifted out of reverse and into low.

"Go, Clinton, go! Go, Clinton, go!" we shouted, sitting up in our seats as he stomped the accelerator to the floor.

The motor groaned while we picked up speed. He rammed the bus into the bank of snow, tires grinding down to the gravel as we broke through the drift.

"Yea, Clinton! Way to go!"

I had stopped shivering by the time Ruby Stai, a third grader, slid into one of the seats. Her father had bought several goats when they found she couldn't tolerate cows' milk.

On the morning that Ruby threw up in the aisle of the bus, Clinton had loaded his dustpan with sawdust from the gunnysack he kept under the dashboard and sprinkled it over the mess.

We pulled down all the windows.

"You're letting all the cold air in," he said.

"We'll gag if we don't get some fresh air," Marvin shouted.

Clinton hadn't paid any attention to Marvin back then. He didn't pay any attention to him now.

The last kids to get on were standing in the aisle as Clinton pulled our bus up to the end of the long line of buses parked on the street in front of the town school. They began shoving their way to the front as the farm kids streamed out of the buses, turning their heads sideways to protect their faces from the wind as they trudged to the big brick building.

I glanced at the back of the bus to check on Marvin. I had never given any thought to watching out for him. It had always seemed to be the natural thing to do. I wanted to hang out with my friends without having to look out for him, but each time I focused on what I wanted, it felt as if it was at his expense.

CHAPTER 9

Pink juice dribbled down my wrists, dripping in sticky splotches onto my shorts as I stripped the skins from the scalded tomatoes and hacked their flesh into pieces. Rims and lids rattled in a small kettle while Mom, her temples glistening, pulled more bulging tomatoes from a pail and dropped them, four at a time, into the large pot of frothing water. She scooped each tomato out as soon as its taut skin had split and piled it into the overflowing bowl next to me.

When she had emptied the pails, I loaded them into our Radio Flyer wagon and dragged them to the garden, where I yanked more tomatoes from the sagging vines while she funneled the chunks I'd sliced into quart-sized Mason jars and wedged the jars into her blue, enameled canning pot.

"Listen to them pop!" she said, smiling as the lids snapped out a tinny cadenza when the jars sealed.

My back hurt. My shoulders ached. I felt like slicing off my arms to get out of slicing more tomatoes.

When it was time to prepare our noontime dinner, Mom turned off the burners. I spread plates and glasses around the table while she peeled potatoes and pounded flour into sirloin steaks before browning them in butter. After gulping down the meal, Dad took his twenty-minute nap while she packed sandwiches and fresh coffee into buckets for Marvin's and his afternoon break. When the screen door slammed behind them, she turned the stove on again, and I picked up my knife.

The instant she said, "You don't have to do any more. You've done enough for today," I slumped in a chair.

I reached for the stack of old *West Central Tribunes* and rummaged through them—Eisenhower signing a bill to make "In God We Trust" a national motto, Nasser nationalizing the Suez Canal—and relaxed into a yawn as Mom loaded a batch of sealed jars into an empty peach crate. She propped the crate on her hip and carried it down the stairway to the cistern room, where she lined up the jars with the other vegetables she had canned.

She once told me she had wanted to go on to two years of normal school and become a teacher.

"What stopped you?" I had asked, surprised she had ever wanted to be anything other than a farmwife.

"My mother said a teacher's work was too hard. She said I'd have to carry wood for the stove and discipline the older boys, some of them bigger than I was, and for poor pay besides."

"So, what did you do?"

"I went to Minneapolis and worked as a housekeeper, and then I came home and married your dad."

I remembered a conversation I had overheard while studying late for a test, when Dad's snoring had been so loud, I heard it all the way upstairs.

"Winston. Roll over," Mom said. "You're snoring."

"Don't wake me!" he said, sounding harsh. "I have work to do tomorrow."

"Well, I have work to do too, and your snoring is keeping me awake!"

"My work brings in our income."

Mom worked just as hard as he did—preparing his meals, washing his clothes, raising his children. Why was his work more important than hers?

On one of their wedding anniversaries, I had watched her stir together his favorite hot dish—hamburger, frozen vegetables, sliced potatoes, a can of cream of mushroom soup. I asked, "Why are you cooking for Dad? Isn't it your anniversary too? Shouldn't you get some time off?"

"Winston is a good provider," she had huffed as she slid the hot dish into the oven. "That's more important than eating fancy food in a fancy restaurant!"

None of the old newspapers interested me, and I did not want to help Mom when she emerged from the basement. I wandered outside and found Mark sitting beside the grain elevator, its long skinny tube hovering over the roof of the granary. Grandpa Peterson had sat down on the doorsill of the granary while he waited for the next load of grain.

As he had already turned six, Mark no longer needed me to care for him the way I had when he was small, but I still entertained him by showing him how to fish for bullheads, screen minnows, and run through the six-foot concrete culvert. I sat down beside him.

Chester turned his tractor, with Marvin standing behind the seat, and wagonload of oats into our driveway. Grandpa stuffed a pinch of "snus" inside his lower lip before hoisting himself up from the doorsill. He bent over his gasoline engine and cranked the flywheel several fast rounds.

"Dagnabbit! This son of a gun!" he said as the engine backfired, belching out puffs of black smoke. "What in tarnation is wrong with this thing!"

After several misfires, the engine settled into a rhythm of small explosions, rotating the belt that propelled the grain up a long tube and into an opening in the roof. Marvin went into the granary to steer the stream of oats into a bin while Chester stood at the back of the wagon and adjusted the flow into the elevator by opening and closing the unloading gate.

As I watched the men, I thought about things Dad had said in the past—"Women aren't cut out for field work." "Women can't handle driving a tractor." "Women aren't suited for working in the barn."

A year earlier, I had asked if I could help with the evening chores. I wanted to work with the cows. I liked their warm, sturdy bodies and the way they watched me with their big, saucer eyes.

"You can do the chicken chore," Dad said, rubbing the stubble on his chin.

I knew he considered the chicken chore to be "women's work."

No matter how slowly I opened the door to the henhouse, three hundred Leghorn hens flew into a frenzy, thrashing up clouds of feathers and filth. They pecked the ones with bloodied tails as they scooted by, holding their heads low as they tried to escape the sharp beaks. The "clucky" hens, trying to hatch their infertile eggs, pinched my skin with their sharp beaks as I slid my hand under their hot bodies. The wire egg baskets, filled to the rim, bumped against my anklebones as I lugged them to the house.

After several weeks, I met Dad on his way to the barn. "Is it all right if I stop doing the chicken chore?" I asked. He didn't say anything, just nodded and continued on his way. I had confirmed what he had suspected all along—that my interest in doing the chicken chore would be short-lived.

Once, as he lingered over a second cup of coffee, I had told him a story that my double cousin Ardell had told me. His mother, Dad's sister Rose, did their chicken chore and used the checks from selling the eggs to buy their groceries. Given the low prices of eggs, he wanted to see if they were making a profit on their hens. He added up the costs—buying the chicks, the feed, the oyster shells—and found they were higher than the money the eggs brought in. When he reported his conclusion to his mother, she said, "That can't be right. I wouldn't be able to buy groceries if I didn't have my egg money!" Ardell chuckled as he told me her response.

When I repeated the story for Dad, he didn't chuckle. "Women can't handle numbers," he said, in his most matter-of-fact voice.

"Dad, that doesn't mean Rose can't handle numbers," I said, bracing myself in my chair. "She never has to pay for the chicks or the feed. She probably has no idea how much they cost."

He twisted his mouth to the side and shook his head, the way he did when he disagreed with what was being said.

"Ardell caught her by surprise. She didn't have enough time to think it through."

He lifted his cup and drank several swallows of coffee.

"Dad, I get straight As in math. I'm really good at algebra. How could you possibly look at me and say that women can't handle numbers?"

He set his cup back in the saucer and stared at the table.

"Don't you remember when you were treasurer of our church? How I helped sort the checks and count the cash and how I totaled everything up each Sunday? And when the deacons came over to balance the books, you let me help them tally up the columns?"

But Dad had said all he was going to say.

During another of our after-supper debates, I asked, "How can you not believe in dinosaurs? Where do you think they get all those bones—the ones they keep digging up in Montana?"

"How do you know the bones are from dinosaurs?" he had said, pulling out his red bandana handkerchief to wipe his glasses. "It might just be a bunch of hooey. And if they're real, how do you know God didn't plant them there as a test of our faith?"

Dad was smart. He had never had a course in algebra but could solve my word problems in his head. I did not understand how someone with a mind as logical as his could believe things that made no sense, how despite physical evidence—dinosaur bones and As in math—he refused to budge from what he believed.

Even so, he appeared to enjoy our debates as I tried to poke holes in his logic, and I enjoyed having his full attention while we argued. When I got a heated response from him or ran into one of his walls of silence, I knew it was time to back off. I once overheard him make a point I had made while he was talking to one of Mom's brothers, and I had tested some of his arguments in my classes at school.

Dad may have gotten a certain satisfaction out of arguing with me, but Mom hated our debates. She interjected distracting comments—"I see Joel has plowed up the yard next to his pig house." Or,

"Clarence finally got out to pick some of his corn today." Dad and I ignored them. Marvin said little while we ate our meals, trudging up to his room and shutting the door as soon as he finished his dessert, excluding himself from our family conversations as well as from our debates.

Despite our arguments, Dad would stop at a store to buy a spool of thread or a tube of glue for me, even though it added time to his trips to town. I once heard Mom mutter to one of her sisters, "I would never dare ask him to do that for me." At the time, I had felt proud, but also guilty, that he would do something for me that he wouldn't do for her.

Chester's shovel scraped across the metal floor of the wagon as he cleared the grain from the corners and scooped it into the elevator. His shirt was stuck to his back in large, wet patches.

I remembered the times he took Marvin and me fishing for sunfish and crappies in Norway Lake. Marvin's laughter had floated above the rented rowboat as Chester's 6-HP Johnson outboard motor spewed smoke while we putt-putted across the lake. His eyes lit up as Chester showed us how to thread worms onto our hooks without stabbing our fingers and how to watch for ripples around our red-and-white plastic bobbers.

"I've got one!" Marvin shouted when a bluegill flapped at the end of his line. "It looks like a big one!"

Dad had never taken us fishing. He thought fishing was a waste of time.

Marvin stepped out of the granary and mopped his sleeve across his forehead. The gasoline engine coughed out several final eruptions after Grandpa shut it down. He tucked another wad of snus inside his lip and sat down on the doorsill to wait for the next load.

Mark and I climbed into the wagon and rode with Chester and Marvin to the field where Dad was pulling our McCormick 140 combine behind his tractor. It scooped up the windrows and swallowed them into its rumbling belly, spewing the stripped stalks out its back end as he drove it down the field. When the hopper had filled with grain, he stopped his tractor and Chester pulled the wagon alongside the combine. I held my foot in the thick flow of oats as it streamed from the tube into the wagon. Marvin and Mark sat in the shade of the wagon as Dad continued down the field. Chester stood a few feet to the side, leaning on his shovel.

Sunlight splashed off the windrows as we waited for the hopper to fill. Crickets and grasshoppers, leaping in high arcs above the stubble, scratched out an undertone of rusty songs. An occasional breeze brought a gentle respite from the August heat.

Earlier that summer, a thunderstorm had drenched the windrows of alfalfa. They had to be turned over to dry before Dad could bale them.

"Dad, how about letting me turn the hay? I know how to drive the 'H,'" I had said, knowing he considered turning windrows to be easy work.

He slathered a chunk of butter over a slice of bread and gulped it down.

"I don't suppose it would hurt to let her try," Mom said, as she passed him the bowl of fried potatoes.

I stashed my lunch bucket in the metal tool case on the side of the engine—the same place the men put theirs—on the smallest of our Farmall tractors. The lugged tires whirled beside me as I turned onto the gravel road and pulled the throttle lever.

Watching over my shoulder, I made certain the rake was aligned with the windrows as I drove back and forth in the field. Back and forth and around the corners. Back and forth and around as the tines of the rake rolled the windrows over. Sweat dripped into my eyes. Mosquitos swarmed around my neck. My legs stuck to the metal seat. The groan of the motor throbbed in my ears as I drove back and forth and around.

The tractor lurched over a windrow, jolting me out of my stupor. I looked back and saw the rake had cut eight-foot gaps in the two windrows the tractor had crossed.

"How can you stand driving back and forth, hour after hour, with the mind-deadening noise of the tractor?" I asked Marvin after parking the tractor next to the machine shed. "How can you stand to have the sun beating down on you until you're sure you're going to die of a heatstroke?"

He grinned as I yanked my lunch bucket from the tool case. "I noticed you had a little trouble with a couple of the windrows."

It was his way of letting me know he had gotten satisfaction at seeing me brought down from thinking I could readily do the work that was required of him. I felt sorry for him because Dad expected him to spend long days in the fields, but I also resented his smugness in watching me bungle what was supposed to be an easy job. I wanted to respond with a sarcastic retort, but I was afraid of setting him off on an endless stream of defensive responses.

I had tired of his grumbling when he had to get up in the morning, his grumbling about the work he had to do, and his grumbling as he retreated at night, shutting the door to his room, shutting me out of his life.

My loss of interest in working in the fields hadn't bothered Dad. I had confirmed what he had always believed—that women can't handle fieldwork.

The tractor started with a rattle as Chester pushed the starter button. Dad had stopped halfway down the field with a full hopper. I decided to walk home instead of joining Marvin and Mark in the wagon.

I climbed through the barbed wire that enclosed our pasture and found a place away from the cow pies swarming with flies. Resting my head on my hands, I lay on my back and watched the plump clouds hanging in the sky above me.

I thought about the way Dad's face had beamed when Betty was crowned Princess Kay of the Milky Way, first for Swift County and then for the west-central region of Minnesota. His broad chest had swelled as we watched her ride on floats with crêpe paper streamers floating above her head and on the backs of convertibles with the skirt of her lime-green dress draped across the trunk. He smiled as he studied the photographs of her splashed across the pages of the *Kerkhoven Banner* and the *West Central Tribune*. I had practiced the side-to-side, beauty queen wave and the open-mouthed, beauty queen smile in front of our vanity mirror, but I could see that I did not have a beauty queen face.

Dad's face never lit up as he glanced at the As on my report cards. "A person can be smart at book learning and not be able to farm worth a hoot," he said about a farmer who spent large amounts of time studying the Bible but barely scraped out a living working his land.

I wanted Dad to be proud of me—to value my achievements, to respect my ideas and the things I did. I may not have been cut out for farm work, but I could get a good education and qualify for a job that would bring in a substantial income, earning enough to support myself and, if need be, a family as well. I would prove to him that a woman can be as successful as a man.

But Dad didn't much care what I did. He expected his daughters to marry good providers.

He was a good provider, buying up neighboring land until he had expanded the family farm to nearly four hundred acres. He had proudly assumed his position of authority as the oldest son, taking on the responsibility for dealing with family matters and for watching over his parents, who lived in the retirement place that his father had built.

Dad counted on continuing the tradition of passing the family farm down to the oldest son—as Ola Pettersson had passed it on to John, as John had passed it on to Dad, and as Dad planned to pass it on to Marvin. He expected him to love the farm as much as he did.

But Marvin did not share Dad's sense of duty as the oldest son. Nor did he share his powerful attachment to the land.

"All farmers ever think about is work," he said as he plodded out the door. "They work from the time they get up in the morning until they go to bed at night."

He hated having to pull a drag behind a tractor to break up the clods of soil left by the disc he had pulled around the same field the day before. Hated forking chopped corn into the silage blower until the silo was filled to its steel-bowled top. Hated having to milk a dozen cows.

"I want a job in town," he said, "a job with decent hours and good vacations."

I happened to have been in the kitchen with Mom the day Dad stormed into the house. His voice had pulsed with rage.

"Where is Marvin? Is he still upstairs?"

"I'll get him," Mom said, tossing her dish towel aside.

"Tell him to get himself down here! We have work to do!"

I fled into the living room and pressed my hands over my ears.

"Why can't he get himself going?" Dad said. "What in tarnation is wrong with him!"

Mom rushed up the steps to rouse Marvin from his bed.

"He's a lazy good-for-nothing!" Dad muttered as he stomped out the door.

Dad had always kept his emotions under a tight rein, restraining his anger in a tense silence. Never had I imagined he would call my brother a "good-for-nothing."

His words ricocheted through the kitchen. They reverberated through the house. Penetrated my heart.

I had felt sick as I scanned the cracks in the plaster above my head, following their jagged tracks across the ceiling. Marvin had never had the courage to stand up to Dad; he took in his disparaging words without responding. Mom shielded him against criticism—other than her own—but she, too, had withered under Dad's attack. I wanted to stand up for my brother, to protect him from Dad's accusations, but I also was afraid to confront Dad when he was angry and did not want to risk my relationship with the father I loved.

After lying awake for several nights, I decided to intervene through Mom.

I waited until I found her alone in the kitchen.

"Can you talk to Dad?" I said, unable to keep my voice from quavering. "I think he's being too hard on Marvin." She looked at my swollen eyes, as if taken aback that I cared about the way Dad was treating my brother.

She did not respond. I never knew if she interceded with Dad.

CHAPTER 10

*M*arvin and I never dreamed the streets of Willmar would be slicked with three inches of snow—the first snowfall of the season—when we signed up to take the driver's test on October 29, 1957, the day of our sixteenth birthday and the first day we were eligible to take the test.

I wanted a driver's license because I no longer could catch a ride with Betty, who had moved to Minneapolis, and her boyfriend, Merlin, when I would sit in the backseat and pucker my lips, pretending to kiss my imaginary date whenever they kissed. I wanted a license so I could drive my friends to the roller skating rink in Benson and skate in circles to "Ain't Misbehavin'" and so I could pack them into our car and go to the drive-in theater in Willmar and slurp root beer and gobble popcorn while squashed together in the seats.

Marvin wanted a license. All the boys wanted to get behind the wheel and fishtail a car down the gravel roads, pound the accelerator and spin the speedometer from zero to sixty in less than ten seconds, and leave a trail of rubber stripes on the concrete slabs of US Highway 12. Six of us had cruised down a deserted highway in Arnie Johnson's 1954 Mercury, staring at the needle as it circled the dial until it leveled out at 113 miles per hour. My heart had raced as fast as the car, but I did not want to be the one who chickened out by asking him to slow down.

On the day I took the test, the officer braced his hand against the dashboard and glanced out the rear window. "*Stop!*" he said. I stomped my foot on the brake. The back end slid in a smooth circle, the car coming to a standstill, sideways, in the middle of the street. When

Dad cramped the steering wheel of our car, spinning it in a circle and making a "doughnut" in the fresh snow, Marvin and I shrieked with laughter and begged for more.

The officer didn't laugh. "You're supposed to *pump* the brakes when you stop in snow," he said, scowling as he released his grip on the dashboard. He docked me ten points for not pumping the brake and hit me with another ten when I failed parallel parking. Even though Marvin and I had practiced next to the log Dad placed in front of our windmill, I was five inches too far from the curb when the officer opened the door. He knocked off a couple more points when my left wheel crossed the centerline as I made a left turn. I was lucky. I passed with one point to spare.

Marvin failed the test.

The officer may have come down hard on him because he thought it was Marvin's idea to put a Hollywood muffler on our 1950 Ford. The cops hated the way the boys rumbled their Hollywoods as they cruised down Main Street. But Betty was the one who had ordered the muffler when Dad sent her to Baker's Ford Garage in Kerkhoven to replace the one that had rusted out. Maybe the boys were right when they said the officers favored the girls. Girls didn't act like they knew everything there was to know about driving when they stepped inside the car to take the test.

Dad did not understand how his son could have failed the driver's test. His anger permeated the silent car as he drove us home.

Most things, Marvin didn't care about, but he cared about driving. He moped around the house for a week before mentioning the test. "Dad thought I already knew how to drive," he said, "because I had driven our pickup around the farm. He gave you more turns to practice. I didn't have a chance to get used to the clutch. That's why I failed."

I locked myself in my room. I had wanted to learn how to slide the stick shift into first gear without getting it into third by mistake and how to release the clutch without killing the engine. I took as many turns as Dad gave me because I wanted to pass the test. Marvin was right—I had been selfish, thinking only of myself. He had failed the test because of me.

Even Dad could see how wretched Marvin felt. Although he had wanted us to learn to drive using a clutch, he let him use our new car, a 1957 Ford with an automatic transmission, when he repeated the test.

Marvin passed with points to spare. He couldn't stop smiling.

When Dad bought a new 1957 Ford, he kept our 1950 Ford for Marvin and me to use as he and Mom had tired of driving to town to pick us up after our school activities. "I decided to spruce it up," he said, handing us a paint brochure when he returned from a body shop. "I sprang for a two-tone paint job."

Marvin and I studied the little colored squares in the brochure and settled on "eggshell white" and "robin's egg blue." I pictured a blue as delicate as the empty shells that floated down from the robin's nest in the eaves of our garage. When Dad retrieved the car, I gasped. No robin had ever laid an egg in the garish shade of aqua that radiated from the sides of the car.

Marvin didn't care about the color. He polished the car with Bee's Wax, changed the filters before the oil got dark, and strewed adjustable wrenches and grease-stained rags across the driveway as he worked on its underside.

The boys at school dubbed our car the "Two-Tone." Marvin grinned as they piled in during the lunch hour. He stuck his elbow out the window and let up on the accelerator, making the Hollywood rumble and pop as he drove back and forth past Bub's Mobil Service, the Farmers Elevator, Swanson's Hardware, and William's Implements. We drove the Two-Tone to school on days when we had games, when I stayed late to edit the *Kerk-Hi-Lites* newsletter, and when Marvin worked on the set and I rehearsed my part as Jane Eyre in our junior class play. We drove to church for youth group meetings, for choir rehearsals, and to go swimming in Lake Florida after Sunday night services. And on Saturday evenings, we drove to the parsonage and picked up David Wickman, my steady, and sneaked into the Willmar Theater where I sat between them, David's arm draped around my shoulder.

We didn't pick a date up for Marvin because he didn't have a girlfriend. When one of the farm girls who had a crush on him sat down beside him in the bus on our way back from an away game, he bolted to another seat. The town girl whom he liked did not like him.

Although David had passed his driver's test on the same day I passed mine, he seldom drove on our dates because the Wickmans had only one car. As soon as he had saved enough money mowing lawns and working for farmers, he bought a seven-year-old, green 1950 Buick, and we no longer took Marvin with us on our dates.

I laughed while the Dynaflow transmission lugged through the gears as David turned his Buick out of our driveway one warm summer evening. The fields of oats shimmered in the late afternoon light. He grinned at me and I grinned back as he turned onto State Highway No. 104, one mile east of our farm. We chatted as he drove past barns and windmills and fields on the six miles to US Highway 12, where we would turn left and, after driving eight miles east, arrive at the Willmar Theater.

He slowed the Buick to a near crawl as we approached the railroad track bordering Highway 12. Squinting in the glare of the descending sun, he glanced both ways. The Dynaflow transmission shifted down to the lowest gear. The Buick began to labor across the tracks.

A horn blared. I gasped as I saw the headlight of a locomotive bearing down on our car.

Steel wheels would have screeched against the steel rails for more than a mile before the speeding locomotive, lugging more than one hundred freight cars, would have been able to brake to a stop. Torches and crowbars would have been required to pry the green metal from the cowcatcher at the front of the locomotive. Hours of searching to find the two driver's licenses so they could identify the sixteen-year-olds who had been in the car. Another hour before they built up the fortitude to knock on the parents' doors.

As it was, the train roared past the back bumper of the Buick. I couldn't scream, couldn't make a sound. David turned onto US Highway 12, and we headed east as the freight cars, going west, rumbled by.

David never told his parents about the train. I never told mine.

CHAPTER 11

E ven though David and I had been steadies for two years, I had never been invited to the parsonage for a family meal—not until our junior year. In late December of 1957, he telephoned me on our party line and said, "My mother wants to know if you can come for dinner Friday night."

I had been inside the large white parsonage, across a small, wooded park from our church, when Mrs. Wickman served coffee and cookies to the church families and when she made hot cocoa for the senior youth group after our skating parties on the pond a short distance away. The house seemed immense, with a long hallway on the second floor and two stairways, one on each end. I was surprised to see so many books lined up on the shelves in Pastor Wickman's study.

When the thrill of Mrs. Wickman's invitation wore off, I began to worry. I couldn't think of anything to say that was important enough to discuss with a minister and his wife. Would I spout something silly, my face blushing bright red, in front of Pastor Wickman? Could I remember to keep my elbows off the table or be able to force down food I didn't like?

After asking God to bless our meal, Pastor Wickman had little to say. Mrs. Wickman passed a platter of fried chicken and a bowl of rice and told us a story: When she and Pastor Wickman were newlyweds, she did not know that rice expanded as it cooked and dumped the entire contents of the bag into a kettle. As it bubbled and frothed and boiled over the top, she divided it into more and more kettles, ending up with enough cooked rice to last a month.

David and I toweled the dishes dry as Mrs. Wickman washed them, after which she said she had something for us. We waited in the living room.

A summer earlier, I had waited for the Wickmans to return from their annual two-week vacation at Lake Nisswa, a three-hour drive north.

The time had passed slowly. I took Mark wading in the stream in Bengtson's pasture; stared at our steers while they stared at me, swinging their tails like pendulums as they swished the flies away; and watched the pigs lounging in the trenches they had rooted in the cool dirt, squealing in loud skirmishes as they tried to invade another's space. I lay across my bed, waiting for a cool breeze to flow through my window, drifting in reveries of David kissing me behind the lilac trees next to the parsonage.

When the Wickmans returned, I compared my pale arm with David's, tanned as dark as his thick, chestnut-colored hair. I listened to his stories of swimming and fishing and waterskiing. When he pulled from his wallet a photograph of Anita, my stomach lurched. I looked at her shiny, dark eyes, her loopy black curls. I pictured them strolling hand in hand along the sandy beaches, kissing as the loons ducked under the water.

"It didn't mean anything," he said, with his teasing smile. "I was just having a little summer fun."

But my lips had trembled when I tried to smile.

By the time Mrs. Wickman invited me to the parsonage, I had stopped worrying about Anita. David flashed his enticing smile as we waited in the living room. When Mrs. Wickman returned, she gave each of us a large box wrapped in white tissue paper. I lifted from my box a blue plaid blazer she had sewn from Pendleton wool. David held up a matching blazer she had sewn for him. We stood side by side and modeled the blazers as Mrs. Wickman checked the length of the sleeves and brushed specks of lint from our shoulders.

The next morning, I pulled my blazer over my flannel pajamas and ran down our stairway.

"Mom, do you like the blazer Mrs. Wickman made for me?" I asked, as I spread my arms and spun in a circle. "She made one just like it for David!"

"Oh, I've heard all about those blazers." She peeled the wax paper from the puff of dough rising above the rim of her bread bowl. "She asked me what I thought about it before she started making them."

"What did you say?"

"I guess I didn't have much of anything to say," she said, punching her fist into the dough.

"Well, do you like my blazer?"

"I guess it's all right."

My blazer warmed me inside as well as outside. Not only did it show David's and my commitment to each other, it displayed Mrs. Wickman's approval of me.

We wore our blazers on our dates and when we sat together at church. Sometimes we wore them to school.

Mrs. Wickman approved of me, but she and Pastor Wickman did not approve of David's behavior. His Buick had given him the freedom he craved. He drove it to town and played pool in the back room of Jack's Café. He smoked cigarettes and drank beer with his friends, sneaked into the parsonage long after the strict curfew his parents had set.

He lost interest in school. His marks plummeted.

When Mrs. Conroy passed back our English exams, David slouched in his chair and snickered with his friends. She marched her stocky body to the back of the room and planted herself in front of his desk, warning him to turn in his assignments on time and to study for the tests. One day she threatened to fail him.

When the class ended, I pretended to be sorting my papers as I watched the doorway. After all the students had departed, I looked at

Mrs. Conroy, leaning over a sheet of paper on her desk, her pen moving down the page, a stack of completed homework beside her arm.

I struggled to keep my voice from quavering as I stood in front of her.

"Mrs. Conroy, I think you're being too hard on David."

Her jaw dropped. With her mouth open, she stared at my face.

My neck felt hot as I stood, paralyzed, before her. I could think of nothing to say, no logic that would make sense, no words to explain my intercession on behalf of a boyfriend who was unwilling to complete the assignments.

Something clicked as I stared at the disbelief frozen on Mrs. Conroy's face. The words I said to her were the same as I had said when I intervened with Mom on Marvin's behalf.

I ran from the room. Ran from Mrs. Conroy. Ran from the glimpse of a self I did not understand.

CHAPTER 12

*E*ven Marvin, who relished food, couldn't stomach the goulash. The hot-lunch cooks plopped globs of the sodden tangle—ground beef and canned tomato soup, glued together with Velveeta cheese—on our plates as we slid our trays past them in the town-school cafeteria. On a late October day our senior year, my friends and I decided to skip the goulash, save our twenty-cent hot-lunch meal tickets, and buy our noon meal at Jack's Café.

As I reached into my locker, David appeared at my side. We never spent our lunchtimes together; he went off with his friends, I with mine. Perhaps he wanted to plan a date for the game Friday evening, I thought, or to go to a movie at the Willmar Theater on Saturday night. I wanted to run my fingers through his thick, fuzzy flattop as he stared at the floor.

"I think it'd be better if we don't go steady," he said.

Clusters of girls were shouting across the hallway, dumping their books and grabbing their jackets. Groups of boys were punching each other while kicking their locker doors shut. I heard but didn't hear.

"What did you say?"

"I think we should go out with other people, not just with each other."

It was David, wearing his favorite charcoal-colored shirt that ballooned out above his belt, the way it always did. But his words made no sense. What could he mean?

"Here's your ring," he said, pulling my class ring from his pocket.

I couldn't think. I couldn't breathe.

"Come on, David, let's get going!" his friends shouted as they bumped their way down the hallway.

He dropped the ring in my hand. It felt cold. Foreign. He was the only one who had worn it.

"And I'd like to have my ring back," he said, cupping his hand in front of me.

I slid my fingers around his ring, cushioned in the groove it had formed in the fleshy pad of my finger. *Did he think it would be that easy—end three years of going steady by slipping a ring from a finger?*

"Come on, David," his friends shouted as they shouldered the door open at the end of the hall. "We're taking off!"

"They're waiting. I've got to go," he said, shoving his cupped palm closer to me. "Can I have my ring?"

I pulled it from my finger and dropped it in his hand. He hurried down the hallway and out the door.

Connie walked up to my locker. *Maybe he wanted more freedom; maybe he felt too tied down.* I pulled on my jacket. *Maybe he wanted more time to hang out with his friends, to party with a faster crowd, spend time with kids who smoked and drank and danced.* Connie walked beside me, down the hallway. I didn't smoke or drink, and I didn't know how to dance; I was happy to ride off in his Buick and have him slip his arm around me at a movie.

We crowded into a booth at Jack's across from Diane and Jean. Jean splashed catsup on her burger. Diane pulled her grilled cheese sandwich into quarters. The ice cubes in Connie's Coke clinked as she stirred them with the straws. Beads of grease oozed from the pink flesh of my hotdog.

No one was saying anything. They knew something was wrong.

My throat felt scratchy. I had to blurt it out.

"David doesn't want to go steady anymore. I gave back his ring."

Connie looked at Diane. Diane looked at me.

"Did he tell you he has a date with Alice for the game Friday night?" Diane asked.

A date with Alice? The words exploded in my head.

"He's been flirting with her in chemistry lab," Connie said. "We wanted you to know, but we were afraid to tell you."

I pushed my hotdog aside and fled from the café.

How could I not have known that he had a date with Alice? With her long dark lashes and curvy figure, she could have anyone she wanted—why did she have to have him?

Alice was Lutheran. She hung out with kids who smoked and danced. Mrs. Wickman would never approve of her. It wouldn't last. Alice would tire of him. Or he of her.

They chatted beside their lockers. I looked the other way.

They sat together at the games. I stopped going.

When they went to a Saturday night party, I stayed at home. Marvin shut the door to his room. I closed the door to mine.

When David called to invite me to a party at Marshall's house, my heart did a jig. But before I had time to say "yes," he said, "I'll be bringing Alice." *What made him think I'd go to a party when he'd be there with her?*

When David and Alice broke up, he dated Joyce.

Joyce was a town girl—a cheerleader with thick, hazel-colored hair and a happy smile. At school, he flirted with her. In church, he flirted with me.

After a Sunday morning worship service, he asked me to go for a ride in his Buick. "I still love you," he said, after pulling over to the side of a backroad, "but I'm not quite ready for us to date." I knew he was stringing me along, playing ping-pong with my heart, but I hoped he'd tire of dating others and return to me.

My misery expanded. It filled my chest, making it difficult for me to breathe. I couldn't talk. I couldn't laugh. When I tried to chat with my friends, I sounded sarcastic. Even Connie got annoyed at me.

When the senior youth group in our church planned an evening of roller skating, one of the town girls asked if she and her friends could come to the party. I told her Pastor Wickman had said the party was to be only for the kids from our church. The town kids came anyway. None of them spoke to me as they skated in pairs, twirling each other in circles, while I skated alone at the perimeter of the rink. They did not speak to me the next day or the next week or the week after that.

After several weeks, one of the town girls asked why I had said they weren't invited to the party. "I'm sorry if I misunderstood Pastor Wickman," I said. She told the other girls I didn't sound sincere.

On my way out of our English class, Mr. Stotts motioned me to his desk. He sometimes handed me a novel—*The Sound and the Fury*; *All the King's Men*—and said, "Here, I want you to read this book."

I had puzzled over one of the questions he had added at the end of my test—"How does the old man's facial twitch serve as a metaphor?"

A twitch was nothing more than the involuntary spasm of a muscle. And yet, it had to stand for something, or he wouldn't have asked the question. Marvin had tics he couldn't control, no matter how much Mom nagged him.

"The old man's twitch stands for things more powerful than we are," I wrote, "things that are outside of our control."

"Excellent!" he had scribbled beside my answer.

But this time, Mr. Stotts wasn't calling me aside to give me a book.

"Forget about him!" he said with a stern look.

"Well tell him to leave me alone!" I said as I dashed from the room, humiliated to have a teacher intrude in my personal life.

During our Social Problems class, I watched the minute hand drag around the clock. When Mr. Nelson said, "Before our sun was created, a twenty-four-hour day didn't exist. Isn't it possible that each of the seven days of creation could have lasted millions of years?" Everyone turned to me, expecting my usual impassioned response to any challenge to my religious beliefs.

But I had exhausted my reserves. Too proud to break down in front of my classmates, I rushed from the room and locked myself in a bathroom stall.

"Marilyn, come on out," one of the town girls said as she knocked on my locked door. "I have a funny joke I want to tell you."

How could I laugh at a joke, when all I wanted to do was cry? I had been dumped by my boyfriend. Turned into an outcast with the popular kids. My relationship with Marvin had degenerated into a string of arguments and insults. What had happened to the brother who lay across his bed, laughing at Woody Woodpecker with that contagious laugh? What had happened to me, no longer wanting to go to school in the mornings?

Instead of waking Marvin, Mom stood in my doorway as I pulled the sheet over my face. "I have a headache," I said. "I don't feel good."

After several days of allowing me to stay home from school, she handed me a thermometer and said, "If you don't have a fever, I'm not going to write any more excuses!" She watched as I ate my cereal but didn't see me throw it up behind the house.

I didn't have a fever, but I knew I was sick. Instead of going to my trigonometry class, I walked out of the school and down the block to the town clinic.

Dr. Helvig, the Kerkhoven doctor, agreed to see me. I described my symptoms, telling him I had been ill for weeks. He took my temperature, palpated my abdomen, and thumped my chest.

"I can't find anything wrong," he said, looking perplexed. "Can you think if there's something that might have upset you, something that could be bothering you?" The instant he asked the question, I put it together. I knew I felt sad; I knew I felt sick. But I had never made the connection.

Mom agreed to come and get me right away. Neither she nor I spoke as she steered the car down the narrow, gravel roads. I hadn't told anyone, not her, not Betty, not Marvin, about the breakup with David. I forced myself to break through my pride and face the humiliation. Digging down, deep inside, I summoned up the courage to admit that I had become sick because of my misery over a boyfriend.

"You probably want to know why I went to the doctor."

My words hung in the space between Mom and me. She nodded, eyes focused on the road. I took a deep breath as we passed by a field of stubble.

"It's because David broke up with me." My voice sounded flat, exhausted, like the shrunken stalks poking up through the snow. "The doctor says that is what is making me sick."

Mom sighed. She turned to me.

"Oh, that's the reason! I thought you were *pregnant*!"

I stared at her, astounded at her assumption, stunned at the relief in her voice now that she no longer had to worry about the stigma of a daughter's teenage pregnancy, worry about the rumors that would circulate around the community, about my having to have a "shotgun" marriage.

Neither of us said anything as she drove the rest of the way home.

She felt relief. But I knew I faced a long and desolate winter.

CHAPTER 13

Dad warmed himself on the bellies of the cows as he sloshed sudsy water over their teats while Mom warmed herself over the double boiler, puffs of steam bursting from between the kettles as she whisked the Cream of Wheat. I pulled the sleeves of my car coat over my hands as the Arctic wind rattled the kitchen window.

"Can't you hurry it up?" I said, as Marvin dumped two heaping spoons of sugar onto his cereal. "Why do you always have to be so slow?"

He lowered his head and scooped up the Cream of Wheat.

"Why can't you ever get yourself going?" I dropped my books on the table and slumped in a chair. "I hate having to be late!"

The snow pirouetted in swirling eddies as he turned the Two-Tone out of the driveway. My toes tingled. I ratcheted the heater lever over as far as it would go. A blast of icy air hit my ankles.

"Why does it take forever for this stupid heater to kick in?"

"Can't you give the car half a chance?" Marvin said, scowling as I whacked the lever all the way back.

"I'm freezing to death!"

"The motor has to warm up before it can put out any heat—you should know that!"

He reached over the steering wheel and rubbed his gloved hand across the frost that had coated the inside of the windshield. A fresh layer of frost trailed his glove.

"I hate this car!" I said as I hunched down in my coat.

"Don't you have any patience? You can never wait for anything! You'd drive any man to drinking!"

I smiled at his hot-blooded retort. A welcome change from his impenetrable grunts and interminable silences. My lack of patience might drive a man to drinking, but his taking forever to get anything done—whining about doing his homework, whining about having to hurry to catch the bus, whining about having to get ready for church—along with Mom's trying to straighten him out and Dad's silent fuming were driving me insane. I couldn't wait to get away from him and his miserable moods, away from David and his string of girlfriends, away from our boring teachers and their boring classes. I was sick of living out in the middle of nowhere where nothing was happening because anything that was happening was happening somewhere else.

I propped my chin on my hand and stared out the window as Mr. Kramer traced his finger down a sine-cosine table in the back of his geometry book while copying the five-digit numerals onto the blackboard. The branches of the trees twisted in the wind as he scraped his chalk up and down, endless lines of numbers trudging behind his hand.

The speaker in the upper right-hand corner of the room squawked and crackled a static-ridden prelude to a disembodied voice:

> "Mr. Lundeen, a recruiter from Augsburg College, is in the room next to Mr. Gulsvig's office. He would like to meet with any students who might be interested in attending Augsburg College…"

Mr. Lundeen had not finished stacking his brochures on the table when I hurried into the room. He explained that even though Augsburg College was located within the city limits of Minneapolis, it provided an easy transition for country kids as most of the twelve hundred students came from farms and small towns. As part of the Lutheran Free Church, it provided a solid religious education, with sixteen semester credits of religion required to graduate. The religion professors not only welcomed debate, they encouraged it.

By the time Marvin had parked the Two-Tone in the garage, I was standing in front of Mom. "I want to go to Augsburg College! Listen to this…" She cupped her hand in a bowl of water and splashed water over Dad's white shirt as I spilled out the information. I stopped to catch my breath before adding, "It's a good religious school, and it shouldn't be too hard to get used to. What do you think?"

"It's fine with me," she said as she rolled the shirt into a cylinder and stacked it on top of a mound of rolled clothes. "But first you'll have to talk to your dad."

After he had eaten several forkfuls of fried potatoes, I listed the reasons it made good sense for me to go to Augsburg. "And Mr. Lundeen says he's sure I'll get a freshman scholarship, and there's more scholarships I can apply for. All I have to do is keep my marks high."

"It's a Lutheran school," Mom said, passing the fried salt pork to Dad. "It's supposed to be a good school. Sheldon likes it there." I knew she was partial to Sheldon, her brother's son.

Dad didn't respond. He focused his attention on a chunk of salt pork.

"You'll have to give us a chance to talk it over," Mom said as she reached for the fried potatoes.

I woke early, rushed to get dressed.

Dad had given his consent.

During my first two classes, I scribbled several drafts of a letter to Mr. Lundeen. After signing out of my study hall to go to the typing room, I rolled a sheet of stationery into a typewriter and clacked out the final version of my letter.

Mr. Lundeen's return letter included an application form. He assured me I would be accepted. I made certain I had included all the requirements when I mailed the application—a photograph of myself, a deposit of fifteen dollars, a personal rating from our minister, and another personal rating from our principal, Mr. Gulsvig.

Each day, as soon as I walked into the house, I sorted through the mail on the kitchen table. When I found two envelopes from Augsburg College, I ripped them open. "Hooray! I've been accepted! And listen to this—'you have been awarded an Augsburg College Freshman Scholarship for $300.00.' That's enough to pay the tuition for one whole semester!"

Mom glanced at Marvin, as if worried that my excitement would make him feel bad. He showed no reaction to my accomplishments; he, too, was able to keep his feelings tightly veiled behind a guarded face. I ignored his silence.

With my acceptance in hand, I searched for ways to pass the summer months between high school graduation and freshman orientation at Augsburg College. I monitored the postings on the bulletin board at school and mailed applications for a science-math institute at St. Cloud State College, a summer fellowship program at the Mayo Clinic in Rochester, and a National Science Foundation program at St. Olaf College in Northfield—all reasonable, as they were within a three-hour drive from our farm.

But I could see no way to escape the winter.

Snow choked the roads. The wind wrestled with the trees.

An icy draft seeped into the kitchen from beneath the door to the entryway, chilling my ankles as I held a bottle of white Karo syrup above my stack of thin Swedish pancakes. The syrup oozed from the neck of the bottle in a fat glob. The glob thinned into a long strand that stretched to the top of my stack of pancakes, where it twirled into a pool. The pool seeped down the side of the pancakes and onto my plate, collecting in a puddle. I dragged my fork across the puddle and watched the tine marks as they faded away.

"If Marilyn is going to college, Marvin should go too," Mom said as she dropped another pile of pancakes onto Dad's plate.

I looked up from the puddle of syrup. *Marvin go to college?* He detested having to study.

"If he wants a good job, he needs a college degree," she said, while ladling batter onto the griddle.

Dad reached for the dish of butter as Mark lifted his glass of milk. Marvin sliced a wedge from his stack of pancakes and stuffed it into his mouth.

The next evening, after passing the bowl of scrambled eggs to Dad, she handed them to Mark, who took a large spoonful before passing them to Marvin.

"Are you going to settle for no more education than I've got?" she asked Marvin.

He said nothing as he heaped eggs onto his plate. I suspected he wasn't sure what he wanted to do, that whatever he settled on would not require a college degree.

"By the time you finish college you'll have a better idea of what kind of a job you want," she said the following evening, while pouring milk into our glasses.

Marvin didn't respond. Neither did Dad, but I could guess what likely was running through his mind—college would shape Marvin up, give him a few years to mature and teach him some responsibility; when he returned, he'd appreciate the farm.

"Augsburg would be a good school for Marvin," Mom said, the evening after that.

I choked on a forkful of pancakes.

"If he goes to the same school as Marilyn, they'll have the same vacations," she said. "They can drive the '50 Ford and ride together when they come home on weekends."

I wanted to say, "Mom, it's not going to work the way you think. I won't be around to knock on his door in the morning, because I'll be living in a different dormitory. I'll have my own set of friends, and I won't be hanging out with him. He'll have to get himself to class on time, because I'll be done—finished with having to worry about him." But I knew better than to say any of that. Besides, she had already made up her mind.

I pushed my chair away from the table, closed the door to my room, and lay across my bed.

Three weeks later, Mom handed Marvin an envelope from Augsburg as soon as he walked in the door. He carried it up to his room. She sprinkled Old Dutch Cleanser on a cookie sheet and attacked the blackened grease with a Chore Ball scrubber. When that cookie sheet gleamed, she scrubbed another.

Marvin clunked down the steps and scraped his chair up to the table.

"What did the letter say?" Mom asked, inky water dripping from the scrubber.

He reached for the *West Central Tribune* and flipped through the pages until he came to the one with the comics. He pulled a chocolate chip cookie from the plate she had set on the table and ate several bites before responding.

"It says I got accepted."

Mom smiled. She tossed the Chore Ball into the can of scrubbers beneath the sink.

CHAPTER 14

A clump of town kids, returning from lunch at their homes, bumped shoulders and flung wisecracks as they shuffled up the hallway. I was relieved to again be included in their activities, making the remaining months of my senior year tolerable. They may have put the entire episode over the roller skating party behind them, but I no longer had any confidence in my friendships. I couldn't wait to start a new life in college.

I glanced their way after tossing my cardigan on top of the teetering stack of books in my locker. I no longer needed it. The fresh rays of the April sun had driven off the morning chill.

"Congratulations," Janet shouted at me. "You're the valedictorian! It's in today's *Tribune*."

My hand froze in midair. *I beat David Smith!*

"And I've been named an honor student!" she said, holding out the sides of her skirt and bowing in a low curtsey.

"Hooray, Janet!" I raised my hands and clapped.

"Let's celebrate," she said. "Let's get a bunch of kids together and have a party!"

"This definitely calls for a celebration." I slammed the door of my locker. "How about we go roller skating. You see who can go, and I'll see if I can drive." Halfway down the hallway, I turned back and shouted, "I'll call you as soon as I get home!"

I grabbed the *West Central Tribune* from our kitchen table and found the big bold headline—"Peterson, Smith, Honor Students"— above photographs of David and me. I scanned through the article:

> Kerkhoven high school's valedictorian of the graduating class is Marilyn Peterson, the daughter of Mr. and Mrs. Winston Peterson.
>
> After graduation the young lady plans to enter Augsburg College, where she will major in science and mathematics. Her interests throughout high school included declamation, girls' glee club, mixed chorus, band, FHA, editing the school paper, [and being a] member of the annual staff and senior class play cast.
>
> The salutatorian is David Smith....

I went back and devoured each word until I heard the smack of an egg against the rim of a bowl. The yolk splashed out as Mom pulled the shell apart. She always read the *Tribune* while she drank her morning coffee. Why hadn't she congratulated me? Maybe she was in a hurry to get a cake into the oven. Maybe she had gotten upset over something someone had said. She could go on forever when she got upset. Even so, I had to call Janet.

"Some of my friends want to go roller skating tonight," I said as she lifted another egg from the can of cracked eggs. "Is it okay if I drive?"

"No." She whacked the egg against the rim. "You've been out too many nights lately. You need to stay home tonight."

What could she mean? I had been out, but it had all been for school activities—editing the *Kerk-Hi-Lites*, rehearsing my part as Mrs. Van Daan in the senior class play, hanging out with friends before the games. No matter how late I came home, I did my homework and got up in the morning without complaining. When I had worked so hard, why didn't she want me to go out for one night of celebration?

Janet would have to plan the party without me. I circled my finger around the dial.

"Can you get someone else to drive?" I said. "Mom says I have to stay home tonight."

"You have to stay at home the day they announce you're the valedictorian? I can't believe my ears. What is *wrong* with your mother?"

The branches outside my window hung motionless against the leaden blue of the afternoon sky as I lay on my bed, wondering what I had done to upset Mom. I always came home before the time she set, knowing how she had worried when Betty came in late. I never challenged her, like I did Dad, as I knew she couldn't tolerate a differing opinion. Never did I sass her back, except silently, when I clamped my mouth shut to keep from saying what I was thinking. I had taken care of Mark so she could go about her work. She couldn't accuse me of skipping church activities, as I went to nearly all of them, even some of the prayer meetings—hardly any of the kids went to them. I sang in the choir, played trombone solos at the worship services, and taught Bible school during the summer. What more did she want from me?

I studied the buds that had puffed up on the branches, ready to burst into their spring finery. Maybe she thought I had gotten too puffed up, that I was bursting with the sin of vanity. Dad didn't worry about vanity. He puffed out his chest whenever anyone complimented him. Maybe he would puff out his chest because I had been named valedictorian. Maybe he had told Mom to keep still about my being valedictorian until he came in from the milking.

I sat up on the bed. That would explain everything! Mom wanted me to stay home because Dad insisted on being the first to congratulate me!

I hurried down the stairway as soon as I heard Dad come in from the milking. He pulled his chair up to the table. I waited for him to speak.

"Did you finish planting?" Mom asked.

"No. I ran into some trouble. If the weather holds out, I'm hoping to be able to finish tomorrow."

"How much do you have left?" she asked.

"I'm just about done with the corn. One field to go. But then I've got the beans to do."

She handed him the platter of pork chops. He buttered another slice of bread. Marvin heaped a second helping of boiled potatoes onto his plate. Mark downed his glass of milk.

I pushed my chair away from the table, saying I had a lot of homework. No one stopped me as I walked to the stairway.

After exhausting myself from crying, I fell asleep.

I pressed a cold washcloth over my swollen eyes before I got dressed. Mom reached into a cabinet for the sugar bowl as I pulled my chair up to the table. My voice sounded as defeated as the words I had rehearsed.

"It seems strange that neither you nor Dad bothered to say anything about me being the valedictorian."

She turned with a start.

"Well, everyone knew you would be the valedictorian."

"How could everyone know something I didn't know?"

"You've been a straight A student for years. Why would it be a surprise?"

"David Smith's been a straight A student for just as long as I have. What gave you the right to think my grades were higher than his?"

"How was I to know he had straight As?"

I pushed away the bowl of cereal.

"I worked incredibly hard—did all my homework every night. I studied hours for every single test. It seems you and Dad could have thought of at least one nice thing to say."

I gathered up my books and sat in the Two-Tone while I waited for Marvin.

When we returned from school, Mom was washing pans in the kitchen sink. Marvin grabbed a handful of cookies from the plate on the table and trudged up to his room.

I had flipped through the *Tribune* and found the comics when Dad turned his tractor into our driveway. He never came home from the field until it was time to do the evening chores unless he had to repair his corn-picker or combine or needed to refill the tank on his tractor. But he didn't drive to the gas pump or to the machine shed. He stopped in front of the house. He likely had come home because he needed Marvin's help. But he didn't ask for Marvin. He stepped up to the table, across from where I sat.

Mom walked over and stood at his side. He cleared his throat twice.

"I want to congratulate you for being valedictorian," he said, in the voice he reserved for important occasions. "You've worked hard. Your mom and I are very proud of you."

My throat seized up as I tried to think of something to say, something to let them know how much their praise meant to me, but nothing sounded adequate. My neck felt sweaty.

"Thank you," I said, after what seemed like forever. "I appreciate it."

Dad started his tractor and drove back to the field.

As soon as I saw the envelope from the National Merit Scholarship Corporation, I ripped it open. "A letter of commendation!" I said, waving it in front of Mom. A letter arrived from St. Olaf College. "Mom, listen to this! A National Science Foundation scholarship for eight credits of chemistry this summer!"

I clipped the articles, "Valedictorian Gets Summer Scholarship" and "Kerkhoven Senior Girl Cited for Brains," from the *West Central Tribune* and the *Kerkhoven Banner* and stapled them into my bulging scrapbook, after the page with the program for the Ice Follies from our senior class trip to Minneapolis. On the next two pages, I fastened the programs for our graduation ceremonies—the Rev. H. S. Froiland from the West Norway Lake Lutheran Church as speaker for our baccalaureate service and Dr. Sidney Rand from the Evangelical Lutheran Church in Minneapolis for our commencement exercises. I reread the letters—"May I extend my congratulations to you on your outstanding scholastic record…"—from Minnesota's US senators, Hubert H. Humphrey and Eugene J. McCarthy, before stapling them onto the following page. On the last two pages, at the end of the row of eleven report cards, I punched the stapler two more times, securing the one from our senior year.

Marvin didn't save any newspaper articles. He threw the information from our senior class trip into his wastebasket, discarded our graduation programs. He tossed his last report card into a drawer in his dresser.

A few days after the graduation ceremonies and a week before I was to leave for the summer program at St. Olaf, Mom walked into the kitchen with an armload of groceries.

"I ran into Mr. Gulsvig while I was in town," she said, as she dropped the bags on the table. "I told him you said the race between you and David for valedictorian was really close."

"What did Mr. Gulsvig say?"

"He said it wasn't that close."

I closed the door to my room and reached into the smallest of the three caramel-colored Samsonite suitcases Mom and Dad had given me as a graduation gift and found the envelope from St. Olaf College. I reread the four pages, "Information on the Special Science Program," and made certain I had packed all the recommended items. Before tucking the envelope back into the suitcase, I rearranged the box of stationery and my confirmation Bible. I snapped the two locks shut and set the suitcase between the medium-sized one, filled with pajamas and underwear, and the large one, packed with skirts and blouses.

After locking my portable Olympia typewriter into its pewter-colored case and placing it alongside the long black one that held my trombone, I lined them all up, ready to go, next to my bedroom door. I couldn't wait to start a new life—to break free from my twin and his surly silences, from feeling dragged down by his endless complaining, his never getting anything done. Like Castor and Pollux, the Gemini twins of the zodiac, we had been tightly bonded. But something had gone wrong.

By the time we graduated from high school, I had lost the brother I loved.

CHAPTER 15

I had watched Mom when she sat down at the kitchen table—putting off the mending of Dad's overalls, ignoring the mound of rolled-up sprinkled shirts, leaving the discs from the cream separator to soak in sudsy water—and picked up her pen. She loosened up her fingers by swirling a slanted coil of loops, a parade of spirals she had perfected in Kandiyohi County School District No. 15 North, spinning them across the back of a discarded envelope or above the headlines of the *West Central Tribune*. She opened her tablet of school paper, which she preferred over stationery. The words flowed through the tip of her pen as she filled both the fronts and backs of the large sheets, numbering each side in the upper right-hand corner.

She wrote to her sister Olga in Minneapolis; to her aunt Ingaborg in Chicago; to her cousin Vivan in Sweden, letters that she wrote in Swedish; to distant relatives after meeting them for the first time; to new friends she had met at a church retreat; and when her children left home, she wrote to each of us.

In the fall of 1959, when we were freshmen at Augsburg College, Marvin and I found her letters, one each week, stuffed into our mailboxes in the mailroom. She addressed the envelopes to both of us; the one who received the letter, after reading it, shoved it into the mailbox of the other. She sent news about our first cousins—all twenty-eight of them—our double cousins, our second cousins once removed, our classmates from Kerkhoven High School, the people she'd talked to at the midweek service at church, Dad's work in the field, and how Mark was doing in the one-room school. Her letters brought me back to wagon boxes heaped with grain, newborn calves wobbling on still-wet legs, the crowing of roosters at the first hint of morning light.

Before Marvin and I left for college, it had been my job to retrieve the letters she received during our summer vacations. The crows cawed a raucous chorus as I sauntered barefooted down the driveway, beneath the overhanging branches of the boxelder trees, to our mailbox. Dad had fixed a sign that said "WINSTON PETERSON," which he had made by screwing four-inch letters onto a slab of red plastic, into the ground next to it.

Mom would sort through the magazines—the Farm Journal, the Women's Home Journal, the *Covenant Companion*—as soon as I dropped the bundle of mail on the kitchen table. "Ah, I finally got an answer to the letter I wrote to my cousin in Sweden," she would say, "it'll take me a while to translate that one!" She pored over each sentence, commenting on the news to whomever happened to be in the kitchen. "Oh no! My aunt Ingaborg has been sick. I wonder if it's the same thing that's been going around here." After she gleaned all the details, she slid the letter into a slot in the wooden letter holder Dad had hung on the kitchen wall. When she wanted to read again about an uncle's impending surgery or the wedding plans of a niece, she pulled the letter from the slot.

Mom's mother, Maria, had continued to live with us after her father, Hjalmar, died, the year Marvin and I turned eleven. She would tie a few of her belongings into a scarf and say, "I tink it's time to go home now," as she thudded her cane across the kitchen floor and out the entry door. After shuffling down our driveway, she turned left, believing her home in Sweden was but a short distance down the gravel road.

Dad waited ten or fifteen minutes before backing our Ford out of the garage. "Would you like a ride?" he asked as he stopped alongside her, knowing she would have tired by then.

Mom steadied her mother's arm and guided her back to the rocking chair in our living room. After bringing her a cup of coffee and a homemade doughnut, her favorite snack, Mom reached into a slot in the letter holder. "Here's a letter from Olga," she said as she handed it to her. When Grandma had read the letter from her oldest daughter, not remembering she had read it before, she would pick up her cane and clomp her way up the stairway for her afternoon nap.

When I opened the letters that Mom wrote to us at Augsburg College, my roommates in the Gerda Mortensen Dormitory, Sharon and Kathy, asked me to read them out loud so they, too, could enjoy the news from the farm. I stopped to interject clarifications—"Mark is nine. I took care of him when he was little. We nearly spoiled him to death!"—as I lay on my bunk bed in our room.

They laughed at Mom's diatribes:

> My problem is someone who has no God, yet uses God's name in vain. If they don't believe in God, why mention Him at all?…I get so disgusted with, "Oh, my God"—if the God wasn't capitalized it could be a car, a beautiful ship or whatever, it wouldn't refer to the spiritual God and I wouldn't think less of them.… when I read "Oh, my God" it sounds like (reads like) profanity to me. I don't admire it.

I did not realize how deeply her warnings about profanity had been ingrained in me until the evening Sharon and Kathy decided it was time for me to get rid of my goody-two-shoes demeanor. When the telephone operator in the lobby buzzed our room to let me know my date had arrived, they blocked the door.

"It's time for you to learn how to swear," Kathy said.

They laughed, and I laughed too, while I tried to shove them aside.

"You have to say 'Shit!' before we'll let you out," Sharon said, as they locked arms to prevent me from opening the door.

Not only did they want me to commit the sin of swearing, the vulgarity of the word they had chosen repulsed me—it suggested an area of our bodies that we had been taught was taboo. My tongue turned into cement.

"Come on," Sharon said. "Just say 'Shit!' and we'll let you go."

My date was waiting. Surely, I could force the despicable word out of my mouth. I silently rehearsed the obscenity, until in one vigorous spurt, I spouted it out:

"*Shit!*"

Discharging the word shattered the muzzle Mom had clamped on my mouth. I tried out the other forbidden words. "Damn it!" I said when I dropped my lipstick. "What in the hell did I do with my billfold!" I said as I exercised my newfound liberation. "Good God, it's cold out!"

When Kathy said we needed to have "smooth lines" while wearing straight skirts, I bought a panty-girdle and admired my sleek behind as I rotated in front of our mirror. I asked a hairdresser at Dayton's department store in downtown Minneapolis to cut off the long, straight ponytail Mom loved and had her perm my hair.

Professor Jordahl, my Basic Bible instructor, stunned me, then electrified me, by saying that the books to be included in the New Testament, after being debated with much contention, had not been fully settled until the fourth century, with the merits of some still in question; that the belief in the virgin birth of a savior was not unique to Christianity, having been a common belief in religions at the time; and that many of the stories in the Bible were mythological, not to be taken literally. I felt as if the bars were being wrenched from the windows.

Near the end of the first semester, I leaned over my desk in our small, cramped room in the Gerda Mortensen Dormitory to consider the letter I was about to write. I thought about all that I was leaving behind—the barn swallows lined up on the power line by the windmill, their cobalt-blue backs glistening in the morning sun; the crunching of gravel under the lugged wheels of Dad's tractor when he returned from the field; the slippery softness of the muskrat coat Mom wore when we went to a dinner party at the home of one of her brothers or sisters.

When the sisters and sisters-in-law had tied on their aprons to wash and dry the dishes and the brothers and brothers-in-law had settled into the living room chairs with their cups of coffee, Marvin and I dashed upstairs to play in the bedrooms. Our older cousins would turn out the lights and tell ghost stories, making us scream by grabbing our necks during the scariest parts.

When I tired of the games, I found the room where the coats were piled on a bed and burrowed into the mound until I found the muskrat coat. I had wrapped myself inside the pelts that carried the scent of Mom, pressing my cheek against the fur until I fell asleep.

I decided to address my letter to Mom, since Dad received ample recognition for his hard work and she received little if any credit for hers. I wanted to express my gratitude to her and my love for her, to secure the bonds that tied me to her, even as I pulled away from her tight hold on me.

After filling six pages with my favorite memories, I copied my final version onto my cream-colored stationery and numbered each side in the upper right-hand corner. I walked down the steep, narrow staircase of the Gerda Mortensen Dormitory and handed the envelope to the telephone receptionist in the lobby, who placed it in the outgoing mail.

Three and a half years later, in June of 1963, I graduated summa cum laude from Augsburg College. Marvin had dropped out halfway through our sophomore year.

He had packed all his belongings in the backseat and trunk of the Two-Tone before picking me up at my dormitory for our semester break.

"Augsburg's not the right school for me," he said, his voice strident as he pounded his palm against the steering wheel. "I can transfer to St. Cloud. They'll take my credits."

His decision did not surprise me. Mom had forced him to go to college. His marks were low. His inability to buckle down and study, his constant muttering and endless excuses, had exhausted my tolerance.

After one quarter at St. Cloud State, he dropped out of that school too, returning home to farm with Dad. He had little to say, disappearing into the barn with Dad and Mark when I brought my college friends home for weekend visits. I seldom saw him during my busy summers—touring to Alaska with the college band, traveling to Italy on a study program, beginning my twelve-month residency in medical technology at the Swedish Hospital. I didn't see him for more than a few days after I graduated from Augsburg, before my roommate Sharon and I had folded down the top of her new black Falcon convertible and driven off on a six-week trip to California.

The wind whipped through our hair as Sharon and I drove across the flat grasslands of the Great Plains, up to Oregon, down to California. We bought potato chips, Peppermint Patties, and Winston and Salem menthol cigarettes. Sometimes we drank vodka tonics before dinner. We went to parties with students we met at the Old Faithful Inn in Yellowstone National Park and with the operators of the monorail trains at Disneyland in Anaheim.

In the postcards I mailed to Mom and Dad, I described the scenery at Crater Lake and the Grand Canyon and Bryce National Park and told them of our visit with Dad's sister in Los Angeles. I did not mention the cigarettes, the vodka, or the parties.

When Sharon and I returned from our vacation, we moved into an apartment near the University of Minnesota Hospitals, where I had been hired as a research assistant by Dr. Wesley W. Spink, an international expert in brucellosis. I was thrilled to be able to work in his laboratory, proud to have been able to identify a difficult-to-isolate bacteria—haemophilus influenzae—in one of his patients during my first few weeks of working for him.

Flush with my successes, I stopped to catch my breath after the mile-long walk from the hospital laboratory to our apartment building before opening our mailbox. When I saw the slanted loops, I knew the letter was from Mom. The thickness of its contents promised a bundle of news.

By the time the door to our apartment had closed behind me, I had slid my index finger under the flap on the envelope, eager to learn how many bushels per acre of corn Dad was getting; if Mark, having started seventh grade, liked riding the bus to the town school; how Marvin was settling into farming. I wanted to know what was happening with the cows and the chickens and the little pink piggies that felt so warm and fuzzy when I cuddled them against my belly.

But when I opened the envelope, the letter it contained was not from Mom. It was the one I had written to her four years earlier, when I was a freshman at Augsburg College. She had returned it with a brief note:

> I've treasured this letter and kept it in a special place, but I no longer want it. You are <u>not</u> the daughter I thought you were!!

The blood drained from my head. What had caused her to return the letter I had filled with my most treasured memories? The words in her note seared into my mind. What I had done that made her reject my love, reject me as her daughter? Did she assume I had driven off to a lifetime of sin when Sharon and I drove off for six weeks of freedom before buckling down to our full-time jobs? Had I become too arrogant with my successes and she felt the need to cut me down?

The letter trembled in my hands as I stood, alone, in my white uniform and white shoes. Alone, in our small, gray basement apartment.

"Talk to the minister if you need help," she had always said when someone felt overwhelmed by their distress. I searched through my stack of old church bulletins from the First Covenant Church in downtown Minneapolis and dialed the number of the minister but hung up before the phone had time to ring. My chest felt tight as I rehearsed my request—"You don't know me, but I've been attending your church and I need help…"—before dialing again. He heard the anguish in my voice but was on his way to a meeting with the deacons and suggested I make an appointment for the following week. What had made me think the senior minister at a large city church would have time to meet with someone, no matter how distressed, whom he didn't know?

I did what I had always done. I dug down, burrowed deep within, until my wound felt less raw. I transformed my pain into something cold and hard, fueled by defiance and resentment, giving me the fortitude to go forward with my life as if nothing had happened.

Two weeks after Mom had returned my letter, I pulled the cream-colored sheets from the envelope and ripped them into pieces. I dropped them, one by one, into a burner on our gas stove and watched them disintegrate into ashes.

CHAPTER 16

The thumping of the tires. It always brought me back. The thumping as the tires rolled over the joints in the two-lane concrete road, US Highway 12, on the 120-mile drive from Minneapolis to the farm. The rhythm slowed every seven or eight miles as we approached the towns—Cokato, Darwin, Dassel, Atwater, Kandiyohi—each with a grain elevator, a smattering of stores, and a daddy longlegs water tower standing guard over the sleepy streets.

The tires of our 1938 Ford had thumped the beat when Dad drove us home from the city after visiting our relatives—his aunt Sophie, Mom's sister Olga, his sister Bernice. Marvin and I jostled each other in the back seat and begged him to stop for ice cream in Litchfield, the halfway mark. We slurped the dribbles as they seeped down the sides of the cones and onto our sleeves.

When I drove my 1950 Chevrolet, passed down from Grandpa Peterson to Chester and then to me, the tires thumped the familiar beat on my trips home from Augsburg College. The cadence soothed me as the concrete blocks of US Highway 12 receded in my rear-view mirror. I knew I would be greeted by the sweet smell of alfalfa permeating Dad's barn clothes, and sometimes by the rancid odor of manure clinging to his four-buckle overshoes, as I bounded up the steps and into the entry to our house.

The tires thumped the years away when George and I drove from the Minneapolis-St. Paul International Airport to the farm with our children, Naomi, Nikolaus, and Stephanie, bumping against each other in the back seat. Dad pulled cobs from shrunken cornstalks for them to shell into two-pound coffee cans while they played in the retirement house where Mom and Dad had moved after Mark took over the farm. He had plugged in the block heater on his tractor and scooped up a pile of snow as a starter mound, then climbed onto the toboggan behind our children as they had plunged down the hill.

But in 1986, when George and I and our three teenaged children flew to Minneapolis from our home in Lenox, Massachusetts, the thumping of the tires ended at the Regency condominium building in Willmar where Mom had moved in 1984, four years after Dad, at age sixty-nine, had died.

I had expected to see Mom's welcoming smile as she opened the door to her unit but did not know Marvin and his seven-year-old daughter, Kristi, would be standing beside her.

I had seen very little of him in the twenty-five years since he had dropped out of Augsburg College. After a couple of years, he had given up farming with Dad and volunteered for the army, serving as an ammunition bearer in Germany.

When he returned from his two-year stint in the military, he surprised Dad by doing exactly what he had said he was going to do. He worked on the farm for a year—"I'll work from 8:00 to 5:00," he told Dad—and then moved to Minneapolis and enrolled in a two-year electronics program at the Northwest Electronics Institute.

By then, Dad no longer cared that his oldest son was not interested in taking over the family farm. Our brother, Mark, who had just turned sixteen, loved the farm as much as Dad did.

I was happy to see my twin and to have a chance to get to know his daughter. But I detested his beard. When he returned from the army, his thin face had been clean-shaven. The year he married Sharon, after he had turned thirty, a manicured mustache outlined his upper lip. By the time Kristi was born, seven years after they married, his bristly sideburns had migrated down his cheeks and across the bottom of his chin. The last few times I had seen him, a rust-colored thicket hid half his face.

It was hard to believe we had once looked so much alike. My favorite portrait was the one taken when we were seven months old.

"Can you tell which one is me?" I would ask my friends.

They wrinkled their foreheads as they studied the two round faces—no hair, no eyebrows, no eyelashes—sitting side by side in matching white outfits.

We still looked alike in the high school portrait that Mom had given to all our relatives—light blond hair, colorless brows, and colorless lashes—his cheek grazing my head. She had placed a framed copy of that photograph on one of the shelves in the television room of her condominium.

The day after we arrived, I was drinking my first cup of tea when Marvin huffed in the door behind George as they returned from an early-morning run through the deserted streets of Willmar.

"The guy doesn't know a thing about circuits," Marvin said, as George reached around him to close the door. "I can't believe they made him the manager!"

George pulled a hanger from the closet and held it out for Marvin.

"We've got a janitor who knows more about electronics than that guy!" Marvin said, hunching his shoulder and throwing out his hands.

A clump of George's charcoal-colored hair strayed across his angular face as he jiggled the hanger in front of Marvin.

"One guy in our department says the manager doesn't know his head from a hole in the ground!" Marvin said, not noticing the hanger.

"Hand me your jacket, Marv. And you better take your boots off . They're dripping all over the carpet."

"A guy who doesn't know anything!" Marvin said, his face flushed as he stuck his hands up in the air.

When he bent down to untie the laces of his work boots, I walked into the kitchen where Mom was swirling her whisk in a kettle of oatmeal.

"He'll calm down when he gets something in his stomach," she said.

Marvin had always loved her oatmeal. He loved all the food she prepared—fried chicken packed with homemade stuffing, rice pudding dotted with raisins, waffles she ladled into her waffle iron, the sweet smell of brown sugar syrup permeating the kitchen. He would prop his elbows on the table—she never managed to cure him of his manners—as he drenched his waffles with her homemade syrup while I had poured white Karo syrup over mine.

Mom glanced at Marvin as he pulled off his work boots. "Once he sits down and eats, he'll feel much better," she said as I carried the bowls to the table in the dining area of her condominium. Marvin followed me and sat down at the table.

The next day, we crowded around the same table for our noontime meal. After we recited our table grace, Mom passed the baking dish of scalloped potatoes with meatballs that she had pulled from the oven.

"My manager can take his job and shove it!" Marvin said, whacking the edge of the table with a hard blow. The milk splashed over the tops of the children's glasses. They stared at their plates. None of them dared speak.

"What would you do if you quit your job at Control Data?" I asked, watching his face from across the table.

"I'd pump gas in Dakota," he said, glaring at me.

"It might get pretty cold—pumping gas in Dakota."

"It gets cold in Minnesota!" he said, his eyes flashing as he banged the table with his fist. "Down to forty below! What's the matter with you? Don't you ever look at the weather reports?"

When Mom bent down to fit the plates into the dishwasher, I noticed her hair had turned completely white, only a few traces of the red that reflected the russets in her muskrat coat when I had leaned forward from the back seat of our 1938 Ford and run my fingers through the silky pelts.

She lowered her voice as I handed her the knives and forks, the same way she had lowered her voice when she sat with her sister Elsie at our kitchen table, sipping coffee before the men came in from the field. I had cupped my ear, straining to hear what they were saying as I listened from the next room—a neighbor had been sent to a hospital because she needed help; a woman from our church, having lost the will to live, had taken to her bed.

Mom looked up from the dishwasher. In that same hushed voice, she said, "Do you think he's having a nervous breakdown?"

I waited until Marvin said he needed to rest and disappeared into Mom's bedroom. After easing the door open, I peered into the room. The bedspread her sister Olga had crocheted hung from a wooden dowel on the wall at the head of the bed. The ticking of her grandfather clock, sitting on the chest of drawers, marked the stillness of the room.

"Marvin, are you awake?" I asked, sliding into the rocking chair next to the head of the bed. "I'd like to talk to you for a couple of minutes."

He grunted, didn't open his eyes.

"I've been thinking about the things you've been saying." The carpet muffled the sound of my voice as I rocked back and forth. "You know, the things you've been telling us about your manager? How he doesn't know anything, the way he keeps aggravating you…"

No reaction.

I rocked a few more times as the gray winter light filtered through the slats of the wooden shade on the window, scattering soft shadows across the quiet room. A crimson ribbon marked Mom's place in her Bible, laying on the small table beside her bed. I watched Marvin's chest shrink and expand with each of his breaths as I considered my words.

"When people get treated like the way your manager treats you," I said, "people can put a person under a lot of pressure…sometimes people get stressed out…like you've been saying you're all stressed out.…"

No movement. No response.

I rocked a few more times.

"Sometimes doctors are good at suggesting ways to deal with stress. Sometimes a doctor, if you went to see a doctor—"

"There's nothing wrong with me! I don't need to see a doctor!"

The vein running up the side of his temple bulged. His hand curled into a fist.

I made our first call for help from a neighbor's phone. "Uh huh," the emergency room nurse said when I told her how Marvin had been frightening us with his strident rants. "Uh huh," when I told her how his nightmares had been keeping him awake at night, that he had trouble waking from them in the morning. "Uh huh, uh huh," as I described how his eyes glazed over as he shouted at people I couldn't see.

"It sounds like he's hallucinating. He probably needs to be admitted."

"But he refuses even to go to a doctor—how will I ever get him to go to the hospital?"

"Then you'll have to call the police. They'll have to bring him in."

"The police? Why can't you send an ambulance?"

"Only the police can bring someone in against their will."

Naomi woke us at 6:00 a.m. by pounding on the door of the first-floor guest room, where George and I slept. We heard the television blaring in Mom's unit as we bolted up the stairway and found Marvin pinning Mom down on her knees, one hand gripping her shoulder, the other clenched around her wrist.

"Pray for forgiveness!" he commanded, as the television blasted behind him.

"Marv. Let her go," George said, leaning over his back. "Come on, Marv. You're hurting your mother."

Marvin's eyes looked red and bleary as he glanced up at George. After hesitating for a few seconds, he released Mom.

He spun around and grabbed Kristi. Clutching her to his chest as if she was an infant, he ran to the elevator, George and I racing down the hallway behind him. I jammed the door to trap him inside the elevator and keep him from escaping to his car, while George leaned over him as he kneeled on the floor while gripping Kristi in his arms. George's glasses fell to the floor of the elevator. Marvin picked them up and wrenched them into a pretzel.

What choice did I have? What might have happened if he had driven off during his hallucinations? What if someone had stepped into the path of his car?

I dialed the police.

Fifteen minutes after I placed the call, Marvin shook hands with the two officers. He introduced himself as they strode into Mom's condominium. We all sat down in the living room.

"So, you're Mr. Peterson," one of the officers said, turning to Marvin. "I understand we've been having some problems."

"Oh no, sir," Marvin said, with a loud, uneasy laugh. "No problems here. Everything is fine."

"I understand there's been some disturbances. You might need some medical attention."

"No. No. Nothing's wrong. I'm fine." Marvin said, leaning back in his chair.

"You haven't been causing any disturbances? No trouble of any kind?"

"No, sir. No trouble here."

The officer looked at his partner. He turned to me.

"Ma'am, we can't take a person to the hospital unless there's a reason." He glanced at his watch. "I don't see that anything's wrong.

We can't just bring someone in. Unless he's a danger to himself or someone else. Which doesn't here seem to be the case."

I looked at our son, Nik, wide-eyed as he stared at the officer; at our daughter Stephanie, her eyes fixed on the floor as she clutched the seat of her chair; at George, who was blinking fast.

The bruise circling Mom's wrist.

"What about this?" I said, as I walked over to Mom and pulled up the sleeve of her blouse.

The officer flinched as he looked at the jagged purple swelling where Marvin had gripped her wrist.

"Did you do this to your mother?" he asked.

"No, sir. That wasn't me," Marvin said, scanning the room. "I didn't do that!"

The officer turned back to Mom's wrist and frowned.

Marvin sprang for the door.

He staggered as the officers landed on him. They dragged him to the kitchen; he dug his heels into the carpet. They twisted his arm up his back; he showed no signs of pain. They clamped his wrists into handcuffs; he braced his shoulders. When they tried to walk him to the door, he dropped to his knees. They hoisted him to his feet and threw a jacket across his back to hide the cuffs. He swatted it off with his chin. Mom and I tried to pull slippers onto his feet. He kicked them away.

"We're just trying to make him comfortable," the officer said with a shrug. "It's pretty raw out there. If he wants to go out in his stocking feet, that's up to him."

The officers stepped out the door, one on each side of my brother, gripping his arms. No jacket. No shoes. Wrists chained behind his back as they strong-armed him down the hall.

CHAPTER 17

Swedes are tough. They don't complain. When things get rough, they "get up and get going." They may have developed their stoical nature and taciturn demeanor in order to get through the long, dark winters in Sweden or because they were taught from an early age to avoid making anyone uncomfortable.

Their fortitude served them well when they settled in the tallgrass prairie in western Minnesota. They brought their familiar foods—*kaffebröd*, coffee bread; *glasmästarsill*, pickled herring; *lutfisk*, whitefish treated with lye—which served as a source of comfort in the new and desolate land.

Some of the Swedish immigrants were fortified by an evangelical faith that emphasized Bible study and a personal religious experience, a pietistic movement that had swept through Sweden during the eighteenth and nineteenth centuries. The evangelicals left their joyous Swedish traditions behind—the Midsommar festival, with garlands of flowers and dancing around maypoles; the St. Lucia Day celebration, with a young girl wearing a crown of candles in her hair; a love of *brännvin* and beer—replacing these frivolities with the discipline of their religious beliefs.

The evangelicals who established our family church—first known as the Salem Swedish Evangelical Mission Lutheran Church—were resolute in their beliefs. For those who had been saved by being "born again," the difficulties on this earth were but a transient trial, their mortal lives but a brief preface to eternal life in heaven. "Take it to the Lord in prayer," they said, when someone suffered from inconsolable grief, only summoning a doctor if a husband had fallen beneath the wheels of his wagon or a child lay dying of black diphtheria. "Go to the minister for help," they counseled those who needed more than prayer.

Born-again Christians most certainly did not seek the help of a therapist. Therapists who had not been saved were tainted by the world. They risked leading a troubled person astray by using psychology and reason rather than looking to the Bible for their guidance. One of the ministers, at what became known as the Salem Evangelical Covenant Church, believed therapists were under the power of the devil.

But in January of 1987, after my brother's breakdown in Mom's condominium, I needed more than prayer and the help of a minister. I fought through a haze of exhaustion as I leaned over the product plans and market strategies strewn across my desk at Mead Specialty Papers. At home, I struggled to think about something other than my brother. The terror of his hallucinations flooded my mind as I lay in bed. The panic in his glazed eyes flashed through my eyes as I stared at the darkness.

"Even though he's your twin, you are not responsible for what happened to him," my friends said, when I described the way he had shattered the glass door with his stocking feet, and when I told them how he had said, "I don't know why they had to be so rough with me," as he pulled aside his hospital gown to show Sharon the bruises that marked his arms, splotched his legs, streaked across his chest.

"You might want to talk to someone," my friends said, looking worried as they studied my face.

By then, Marvin had been transferred to the psychiatric ward at the St. Paul-Ramsey Medical Center in St. Paul, not far from their home in Forest Lake. After his release, Sharon wrote, "some people overreacted." I felt as if she had driven a spike into my heart. How could she think I would have called the police if there had been any other way to keep my brother from hurting someone?

My Swedish stoicism was not enough to keep me from falling apart. I needed a therapist.

I looked both ways, worried someone I knew might see me, before slipping into the doorway in the brick building next to the Stockbridge post office, a two-mile drive from my office. After hurrying down a long hallway on the second floor, I opened the last door on the right and stepped into an empty waiting room. I pulled a copy of the *New York Review* from a pile of magazines and pretended to be reading it as a sound machine beneath the table emitted a continuous hiss.

I had arrived ten minutes early. Ten more minutes to worry about what to say to a therapist.

"Sit anywhere you like," Dr. Lippmann said, as I surveyed the chairs surrounding a low, square table in the middle of his office. He pointed at the chair next to the couch. "Except this one. This is where I sit."

After choosing a chair on the side of the table opposite him, I wondered if I should have taken a place on the couch; if shaking hands with him might have been inappropriate. Silly.

"I'd like if you called me Paul," he said, watching my face with his dark, somber eyes. "Why have you come?"

I scanned the hangings on the walls, the books on his shelves, the notepad he held in his lap, his curly black hair, his angular face. I had no idea where to start or what to say to a Jewish psychoanalyst from New York City when I wasn't sure what my story was or where it began. What should I tell him of an expanse of fields under an immense sky? What could he know of twins who stepped into a one-room school, having only had each other?

Steadying myself in my chair, I was determined to maintain my composure, keep everything professional. I told him about my brother's glazed eyes, our chase down the hallway, the way he wrecked George's glasses. When I got to the part about the shattered glass door, I managed a quick laugh.

"You can't believe how strong my brother is. He's like a bull…"

He pointed at the box of tissues.

"Don't mind me." I said, as I pulled a wad of tissues from the box. "I cry at everything. Funerals, movies, I even cry at weddings…"

"Some of my patients cry their way through therapy."

At the end of the session, he followed me to the door.

"Will you be all right?" he asked.

"I'm not sure what you mean."

"You're so full of sadness. I'm worried about your drive home."

"Don't worry," I said with a toss of my head. "I'm strong. I don't want to die."

But as I walked down the long hallway, I wondered what he had heard that made him worry about the depth of my sadness.

CHAPTER 18

loved the expanse of the sky, the way it dwarfed the flat terrain, the way the sunlight glistened off the blades of a windmill, its steel skeleton rising above a small grove of trees. I loved how the wind rippled in waves through the wheat, how it rustled the tassels of corn above our heads as Marvin and I followed Dad down the rows to see how many inches the stalks had grown since we followed him a few nights earlier. I loved the loud flapping of a pheasant's wings, shattering the silence as it lifted off from its nest near a pile of rocks. The touch of the long, cool grasses at the end of our lawn as I lay on my back and listened to the stillness of what had been a tallgrass prairie.

But the stillness camouflaged a violence that resided within the wide sky, dwelled beneath the swaying grasses.

The prairie had been birthed through cataclysmic explosions of molten lava that welled up the Rocky Mountains, cutting off the rain to the east; by mountains of ice that sheared the land and made it flat; and by fires set by the Plains Indians—Cheyenne, Comanche, Dakota, Arapaho—creating infernos that incinerated everything that flourished in the fertile till that had been dumped in the wake of the glaciers. Only the deep roots of the grasses survived—switch grass, Indian grass, big bluestem—creating a massive grazing land for elk and white-tail deer and thirty million bison.

Explorers arrived, seeking adventure and to lay claim to the land. Traders came to trade for furs, missionaries to convert and civilize the Sioux. Surveyors brought compasses and transits and levels and partitioned the tallgrass prairie into a checkerboard of square miles running north and south and east and west. Settlers followed the explorers.

The settlers from Sweden left their home country because of the pitiful wages and the backbreaking work on the farms. They left because they had been squeezed onto tiny plots of stone-ridden land as the population doubled between 1750 and 1850. They left due to repeated crop failures, the inequality of the classes, and the hostility of the Lutheran State Church to the evangelicals, who spurned the formal and highbrow services. They departed because the age of steam had led to vast shipping lines—Inman, Cunard, White Star—which drove down the price of tickets and decreased the length of the ocean voyage from months to weeks. They immigrated to the United States because Abraham Lincoln signed the Homestead Act on May 20, 1862, with a promise of free land.

The Swedish immigrants found jobs in factories in Illinois and Minnesota and Wisconsin. Thirteen- and fourteen-year-old girls, straight from the fields, got off the trains in Chicago and worked as live-in housekeepers. Families with small children trekked to the tallgrass prairie in wagons pulled by oxen, their trunks packed with clothing, basic provisions for their journey, and the family Bible. Before the departures ended, 1.2 million people, more than one-fifth of Sweden's population, had left for the Land of Promise.

Two of the Swedish families were the first white people to settle in Swift County, adjacent to Kandiyohi County. They arrived in 1861.

A decade earlier, the Sioux had ceded twenty million acres to the United States government for promised payments of $1,665,000, retaining strips of land on either side of the upper Minnesota River as a reservation.

But the Dakota, a band of the Sioux, did not receive the annuity payments they were promised. They suffered from failed crops. Their children were starving. Their leader, Little Crow, decided to drive the white settlers out of the Minnesota River Valley and take back what had been their land.

They attacked the two Swedish families, after they had set out for a worship service at a neighbor's cabin. They tomahawked the younger children, who had remained at home. Tomahawked the women and the older children when they returned in an oxcart. Tomahawked a ten-month-old boy, hacking him into pieces in the sight of his mother. Thirteen members of the two Swedish families were massacred. Only two in the settlement, both children, escaped.

The Dakota killed the mail carriers, the stage drivers, the military couriers who tried to reach the settlements. They severed heads and hung them on posts. They nailed infants to trees. By the time the Dakota War of 1862 ended, four months after it began, the Dakota had slaughtered eight hundred settlers and burned many of the settlements in the Minnesota River Valley.

More than three hundred Dakota men, women, and children died of infectious diseases while they were being held in Minnesota prisons. Thirty-eight Dakota men, tried in cursory trials, were hanged in a single mass execution. When a white settler shot Little Crow while he and his teenage son were gathering raspberries, the usual $200 bounty for a dead Dakota person found within Minnesota was increased to $500. The remaining Dakota were expelled from Minnesota. All the settlers were cleared from the area.

In 1869, four years after setters were again allowed in the region, Ola Pettersson, Dad's grandfather, arrived in Kandiyohi County. The land he claimed lay five miles south of the two shallow cellars, the only remaining traces of the two Swedish families.

Marvin and I wondered why Dad fell into a long silence when we stood beside two indentations in the ground, overgrown by a tangle of grasses. We did not know his grandfather had arrived so soon after the many deaths. That the soil Dad tilled, the earth he loved, had been stained by the blood of the Dakota, by the blood of the first Swedish settlers.

One year after Ola arrived in the Land of Promise, the St. Paul and Pacific Railroad slashed through the Indian grass and the big bluestem and the orange coneflowers, slicing a path across the belly of Minnesota as it lay rails heading west. The locomotives belched cinders and plumes of smoke as they thundered across the land where the Sioux had ridden mustangs alongside rivers of bison. The settlers welcomed the trains. Until then, they had no means of distributing their crops. The locomotives lugged their wheat to the cities in the east and returned carrying plows and saws and axes.

Three years after the trains rumbled in from the east, the Rocky Mountain locusts blackened the sky as they flew in from the west. They stripped everything that was green—stalks of corn, blades of wheat, leaves on the trees. The settlers were poor with no means to survive a loss of their crops. They sold their oxen, sold their wagons, mortgaged their farms. Many abandoned their homesteads and searched for jobs.

Two years after the Rocky Mountain locusts departed, an epidemic of "black diphtheria" devastated the region. The doctors worked day and night, but their treatments did not cure the sick.

Eighty children in Kandiyohi County died. Ten of the eighty attended the Salem Swedish Evangelical Mission Covenant Church. Seven of the ten belonged to the Lofgren family. Only one of their eight children, Ferdinand, had survived.

I did not know about the invasion of locusts or the diphtheria epidemic until, as an adult, I read about them in a historical book published by the church. I wondered how the only one of eight Lofgren children who survived had been able to go on.

I asked Mom if she knew Ferdinand.

"When I was young," she said, "he was an old man who sat in one of the back pews."

CHAPTER 19

It made no sense. Why would five of six sisters have left home when they were so young? I puzzled over the reasons as I lined up the portraits of the Larsdotter sisters on Mom's dining area table. Why would they all go off to begin a new life in an unknown city in a foreign country with a language they didn't understand? And yet, each had stepped off a train in Chicago to work as a housekeeper. In the portraits, taken in Chicago, they wore similar dresses—long-sleeved and high-necked, a line of buttons down the front, a long skirt that ballooned below a cinched-in waist—as they posed beside an ornate pillar or next to an Edwardian chair.

Mom's mother, Maria, the fifth of the six sisters, was fourteen when she arrived in Chicago. When I was fourteen, I had felt lost as I stepped off the school bus at the town school, seven miles from our home. When our children were fourteen, they relied on us for nearly everything.

I studied the portraits of the sisters' parents—their father's fair features, their mother's somber eyes in a handsome face. Their photographs had to have been taken in Sweden, as they had never traveled to America to visit their many daughters.

"I wonder what their mother must have thought," I said, as Mom glanced at the portraits while stepping out on her balcony to water her geraniums. "She must have been heartbroken to have her daughters go off like that, leaving her behind, and to such a faraway place."

"My mother never talked about it."

Her mother never talked about it because they had learned to hide their secrets behind a wall of silence. Silence about money. Silence about their sadness. About sex. Unwilling to admit to a weakness, a failure, a need for assistance.

Marvin never told me about the speeding ticket he was issued shortly after he got his driver's license. Mom and Dad never mentioned it. He didn't tell me about the accident he had in Minneapolis the year he was at Augsburg College. Decades later, when I first heard of it, I asked Mom what she knew about it.

"It wasn't good," she said.

Her sour expression had told me that was all she was going to reveal.

Mom was in her mid-seventies when I again lifted the portraits from the basket, where she stored them, and arranged them on the table. The dining area was quiet, the afternoon sunlight soft in a clear sky outside the patio doors. She stood nearby, watching me, as I puzzled over the faces.

"It just seems strange that all the sisters would leave home when they were so young," I said. "There had to have been some reason— something that wasn't right."

She dropped her gaze to the floor, hesitating before she responded.

"I guess their father wasn't nice to them."

I sat up in my chair.

"When did you find that out?"

"I learned it the last time I was in Sweden."

"What does that mean, he 'wasn't nice to them'?"

Her face flushed. She dropped her voice to a low tone.

"I guess he *drank*."

She had not learned of her grandfather's drinking from her mother, who never spoke of it; had not learned of it from her mother's sister Charlotta, who lived with their family the entire time Mom was growing up; did not learn of it from the sister Ingaborg, who remained in Chicago; not from the sister Anna-Kajsa, who moved to Canada; not from the sister Sophia, who lived in Minneapolis; not from the sister Eva-Maria, who had gone back to live in Sweden;

not during their many visits or the multiple letters they exchanged. Only when she went to Sweden and spent time with the family of the six sisters' only brother, Anders, who had remained behind, did she learn of her grandfather's drinking and his abusive treatment of his daughters.

Mom had been raised to believe that drinking any form of alcohol was a sin. Even the church's communion glasses were filled with grape juice rather than wine.

When I was young and our Sunday school teacher told our class the story of Jesus's miracle at the wedding in Cana of Galilee, I had raised my hand. "If drinking is a sin," I asked, "why did Jesus turn the water into wine?"

"He didn't turn it into wine," she said, frowning her disproval at me for my impertinent question. "He turned it into grape juice."

Even so, I hadn't been able to understand why the Bible used the word wine when it meant grape juice.

Decades later, during one of Mom's visits to our home in Lenox, she had watched me sip a glass of wine with several of our friends. After she returned to her condominium, she clipped a column about drunks who sat begging on the curbs in Manhattan until they had enough money to buy another bottle of Thunderbird wine.

She scrawled in the margin, "I'm glad I never took the first drink!!!" and mailed it to me.

At the time, George and I laughed. But I had felt the sting of her scorn.

When Mom confessed that her grandfather drank and was abusive to his daughters, I saw the depth of her humiliation and the intensity of her shame. I felt sorry for her. But I also took satisfaction in seeing her feel the hurt of the disdain she so freely dealt out to others.

Two years before Mom's father, Hjalmar Jonsson, was born, his infant brother had died. A three-year-old brother died when Hjalmar was five. His mother died from tuberculosis, known as consumption, when he was seven. An infant sister died, also of tuberculosis, several months after their mother's death. By then, the family had suffered four deaths.

In 1882, when Hjalmar was eight, his father, Karl Jonsson, and his four surviving children immigrated from Sweden to Kandiyohi County. They lived with Karl's brother for a year, until Karl found a nearby farm to buy. He married the woman who had helped him care for his children, settled his family into the sod house that came with the land, and began a new life.

But Hjalmar had more deaths to endure. Two years after his father had remarried, he fell under a hayrack while trying to restrain his startled horses. He died a few days later. His wife was pregnant with their second child. Hjalmar, his oldest son, was twelve.

As if Hjalmar hadn't withstood enough deaths, the older of his two half-sisters, Lydia, became ill with tuberculosis and died when she was twelve and he was twenty-three.

Hjalmar had established a mail correspondence with Maria Larsdotter while she was working in Chicago. She accepted his marriage proposal when he was twenty-four and she was twenty-seven. He did not have $775 to buy the farm from his stepmother, but Maria made the purchase possible by contributing $300 she had saved while working as a housekeeper.

After they married, Maria moved into the sod house with Hjalmar and his family. With the help of his brother and a cousin, he built a house with four bedrooms and a bay window for Maria's houseplants.

But Hjalmar had yet another death to endure. His other half-sister, Emma, had also become weak from tuberculosis. His stepmother propped pillows in a chair in the kitchen of their new house so Emma could spend time with the family.

Perhaps Hjalmar loved Emma with a special love because her birth had been a gift of life passed on to them after his father's death. He may have felt as if he had filled the role of a father in her short life. It might have been because her happy nature had brought a ray of sunshine into their sod house.

Emma died in 1900, when she was fourteen and Hjalmar was twenty-seven. He poured his grief into a poem:

> O Emma du hafver oss lemnat
> Och gått till ett skönare land…

Mom said her translation—"Oh Emma, you have left us / And gone to a more beautiful land…"—did not capture the music of the Swedish language. But his words captured his sense of overwhelming loss, a culmination of the many losses in his life.

After I learned of the many deaths in her father's family, I asked her what she knew of them.

"Dad never spoke of them," she said.

Maria was forty-three by the time she gave birth to Mom, the last of their nine children, born within fourteen years. "My mother was worn out by the time she had me," Mom said.

In one of her letters, she wrote:

> Maybe that's why she never baked me a cake, bought me a gift, or even wished me a happy birthday. I don't think she ever wanted me but I made it anyways.

Mom walked a half mile across a neighbor's field, along with her many brothers and sisters, to complete the eight grades in their one-room country school, Kandiyohi County School District No. 15 North. "I wasn't smart," she said, "but I was good at geography and spelling."

In order to attend high school, she stayed in the upstairs of a house in Kerkhoven, as the school district did not yet have buses. She and two friends slept in one bed. They brought food from home and cooked all their own meals.

The only one of Hjalmar and Maria's nine children to finish high school, Mom wanted to go on to "normal school" and become a teacher. But her mother discouraged her by telling her the work would be too hard and the pay too poor. Instead of becoming a teacher, she went to Minneapolis and worked as a housekeeper and nanny. She returned to marry Dad when she was twenty-one and he was twenty-four.

Mom wore a slim, hand-sewn, celery-green ankle-length satin dress and a veil that fell into a long train for their wedding in what was then known as the Salem Swedish Evangelical Mission Covenant Church. Dad wore a dark suit and a black bowtie.

She knew the house Dad had rented, the "old Holmberg place" where his mother had grown up, was cold and drafty. He bought a Monarch range, large enough to store an armload of wood, which had a reservoir that heated nine gallons of water and an oven with a temperature indicator. They bought a bedroom set, a table and several chairs, a cream separator, and a radio powered by a battery, as the house did not have electricity. Each morning, Dad drove his green 1929 Chevrolet down the long driveway and around two sides of the square mile to work with his father on the farm Dad's grandfather had homesteaded.

It fell to Mom to feed their livestock—six cows, two white horses, and twelve pigs—which Dad had earned by working for his father. She changed into her chore clothes before feeding the pigs because they splattered the slop in their battles to get the most. In the evening, she pitched hay into the mangers for the cows and horses, throwing six cobs of corn over the fence for each of the pigs. But she refused to milk the cows. "I was not a milkmaid," she said.

They lived on the old Holmberg place for two years, until Betty was two months old, and then moved across the square mile to live with Dad's parents and his brothers. A year later, his parents moved into the retirement house, after his father had finished building it.

Three years later, Marvin and I were born. Mom had two infants and a four-year-old to care for, in addition to her normal farmwife chores.

Part of her work was to feed the threshing crew—Dad, his father, his brother Chester, and eight or more men from neighboring farms.

At 9:00 a.m. she filled a picnic basket and her two metal dishpans with food—sandwiches with bologna or Velveeta cheese on home-made bread, chocolate chip cookies she had baked, slices of a sheet cake she had filled with chocolate and rolled into a log, thermoses of steaming coffee brewed in a metal coffee pot on top of her stove—and loaded them into our 1938 Ford.

Marvin and I rode along because we were too young to be left at home. While Mom spread the lunch out on blankets in the shade of a small woods, we watched the horses as they snorted, pawed their hoofs in the stubble, and flicked their tails to swat away the flies. We stared at the belts that rotated the pulleys on the threshing machine, at the clanging chains; at the straw as it flew out of the long, fat tube, piling up into a tall, golden stack; at the long, wide belt stretch-ing from Grandpa's steel-wheeled McCormick-Deering tractor to a huge pulley on the side of the noisy machine.

At 12:00 noon, Grandpa shut down the threshing machine and the threshers gathered at the picnic table next to our house for the dinner Mom had prepared—scalloped potatoes with ham, corn pud-ding, apple pies, slices of chocolate cake, and multiple thermoses of coffee she had brewed.

When 3:00 p.m. arrived, Marvin and I again climbed into the car as she delivered afternoon lunch to the threshers, much the same as the lunch she had brought to them in the morning. We watched them fork bundles from the hayracks into the long jaw of the threshing machine, pulleys clanking, belts churning, as the screens shook the kernels of grain free from the chaff.

After two and a half days, when all the bundles of grain had been gathered from the fields, Grandpa had hitched up the threshing machine to his steel-wheeled tractor and lugged it to the next farm, and Mom had gone back to her normal load of farmwife work.

I chose medical technology as my major, since I loved everything having to do with medicine. But I had never given serious thought to becoming a doctor until a chemistry professor prodded me—"Anyone can be a housewife, but you have the potential to become a doctor…"—to consider going on to medical school. To go forward with such a momentous decision, I needed Mom and Dad's emotional support for what would be years of arduous training.

When I told them I was thinking of applying to medical school, Dad pressed his lips sideways and shook his head.

"You have enough education," he said.

Mom wrinkled her forehead and frowned.

"The work would be too hard," she said.

Instead of going on to become a doctor, I worked in a research laboratory at the University of Minnesota Hospitals. Years later, I realized those were the same words her mother had used to discourage her from going on to become a teacher.

I was twenty-two and Mom was fifty when Dad drove us to New York City to see the 1964 World's Fair. George's parents had invited our family to stay with them at their home in Lynbrook, Long Island. I had met him two years earlier, when General Electric sent him to Minneapolis on an assignment as a field engineer. Partway through our stay at his parents' home, George proposed.

I flashed my engagement ring in front of Mom. "Look how big it is!" I said, proudly showing off the diamond, six-tenths of a carat, by tilting it back and forth in a beam of sunlight.

Mom frowned as she looked at my ring.

"Remember," she had said, "you're the daughter of a *dirt* farmer."

Fourteen years after I graduated from Augsburg College, I told Mom I was going on to graduate school. I had been changing diapers and chasing toddlers while activists were establishing women's shelters and rape crisis centers and battling sex discrimination in the workplace. I knew I needed to divert my competitive spirit and need to achieve into my own aspirations, rather than living vicariously through our children.

Mark had taken over the farm five years earlier, at which time Mom and Dad had moved across the road into the retirement house.

Dad worked alongside Mark while Mom continued with her usual work, tending a vegetable garden, mowing the lawn, patching Dad's overalls. By then she had worked forty-two years as a farmer's wife.

"Why are you going on to more school?" she wrote, when I told her I was taking evening courses to earn an MBA from the University of Massachusetts. "Mothers need to stay at <u>home</u> with their <u>children</u>!!!" After I graduated and accepted a full-time position as a financial analyst at Mead Specialty Papers, a ten-minute drive from our home in Lenox, she became even more adamant. "Mothers should stay at <u>home</u>!" she wrote. "<u>Teenagers</u> need to have a parent at home, just as much as small children!!"

I tried to ignore her disparaging words, but they had worn me down. "Mom, you always say how good it is for Betty and Sharon to work," I said. "Why do you tell me I should stay at home?"

She thought for a moment. "Because you don't *need* to work."

She had more than made up for her mother never giving her a party by giving so many parties for Marvin and me. She had cut out tails for pin the tail on the donkey, baked double-layered cakes with seven-minute frosting, written sing-song poems as clues for treasure hunts that took us from our pig house to the windmill to the pump house by the retirement house, and been as excited as we were when our guests began to arrive.

Her mother had discouraged her when she wanted to go on to normal school. Why didn't she make up for her mother's lack of encouragement by supporting me when I wanted to go on to medical school? What kept her from being happy for me when I earned an MBA?

CHAPTER 20

Dad's grandfather, Ola Pettersson, had taken on the responsibility for his father's debt and worked it off by the time he was fourteen. Their family had moved from town to town while working for food and shelter, living for a time in the poorhouse on the outskirts of their parish in Sweden. Ola did not emigrate until 1869, when he was twenty-two and his parents had died.

Eight years after Ola, known as Ole Peterson in the new country, arrived in Kandiyohi County, he married Beret Johannes Dotter, who had emigrated from Norway a year earlier. He homesteaded eighty acres of the tall-grass prairie in Kandiyohi County and bought another adjacent one hundred and sixty acres in Swift County. Dad's father, Carl Johan, known as John, was their oldest son.

John and his five siblings walked one and a half miles to the first log school, Kandiyohi County School District No. 54, which the settlers built in 1883. They squeezed two into each desk as they learned to read and write the English language.

John was seventeen years old when he and his father were unloading a sack of wheat at the grain elevator in Kerkhoven, and the spring seat at the front of the wagon fell on the backs of their horses, causing them to bolt. John jumped from the wagon, but Ole was thrown to the ground. He died two days later, at age fifty-two, leaving his wife without a husband and their six children without a father. John took on the responsibility for the farm, his mother, and three younger siblings.

Dad's mother, Britta Holmberg, had not yet turned two when her parents, Per and Karin Holmberg, stepped off the train in the town of Kerkhoven. Karin had wept when Per told her they were leaving Sweden. The long trip had been arduous, Per lugging their trunks of goods and clothing and with seven children to care for, the oldest of whom was nine.

They were taken aback by the desolation of the dusty town, empty of people, with only one store. As they rattled over seven miles of dirt trails in a red lumber wagon pulled by a team of horses, they were shocked by the scarcity of inhabitants. A few dugouts could be seen in the vast flat expanse of tall grasses, an occasional cluster of trees that had been planted by the pioneers.

After living with Karin's sister and her family for a year, Per acquired a farm, kitty-corner across the square mile from Ole Peterson's homestead place, and built a house to replace the two-room log cabin that came with the land. They had five more children.

Dad's mother, known as Bertha, along with her many siblings, walked one mile to the first log school, District No. 54.

Bertha was twenty-seven and John was twenty-six when he proposed marriage. Tall, handsome, hardworking, and with the honor and authority of being the oldest son, he was looked upon as a "good catch."

Bertha wore a long gown with layers of ruffled lace and a flounce atop her upswept hair. John looked stately in a black tailcoat and white bow tie, white gloves draped in his left hand. Their many brothers and sisters and their families attended the wedding, held at the Holmberg home.

John and Bertha had seven children. Dad was their oldest son.

On New Year's Day of 1924, Bertha decided they would visit the family of one of her many brothers. Dad's father, John, stayed at home to take care of the livestock, as although it was a sunny day, the temperature had not risen above twenty degrees below zero. Dad hitched their team of horses to the bobsled. His sisters and brothers climbed in with him and his mother, and they set out on the three-mile journey across the snow-covered fields.

When they arrived at a junction of two trails, they selected the wrong one. Dad turned the horses back to take the correct trail, but his mother and several of the children decided to walk the remaining half mile to her brother's place. Dad looked back and saw she had collapsed in the subzero weather. He made a fast turnaround and carried her to the bobsled.

After their visit ended, Dad guided the horses as they returned to their home. He was twelve years old.

Dad earned high marks at District No. 54, in the new building constructed in 1900, even though he missed several weeks in the spring to help his father with the planting, and again in the fall, when he helped with the harvest.

When Dad had completed the eight grades, he enrolled in a two-year program at the West Central School of Agriculture in Morris, forty miles northwest of their farm, where he learned how to repair machinery and wire for electricity.

After six months at the school, his parents called for him to return home. His brother Chester, ten years younger than Dad, had become severely ill with diabetes. They needed Dad's help. Dad never returned to the agricultural school. He was sixteen years old.

Dad never told Marvin and me about the day he rescued his mother in the frigid weather. He never told us the reason he dropped out of the agricultural school. I had thought he left because he figured he already knew everything he needed to know about farming.

Marvin and I went after the roosters. "Daddy! Daddy! I've got one!" I shouted. It raised a cloud of dust with the wild beating of its wings as I grabbed its leg while it scrambled up the chicken-wire enclosure attached to the henhouse. Dad stuffed it into the wooden crates with the other roosters, their waddles flaming red as they stuck their heads out between the slats.

Grandpa Peterson and Chester had helped us when we lined up in a long row across the woods and waved long branches to chase the young chickens, screeching and flapping their wings, out from among the trees and into the henhouse.

The next morning, we formed a line behind the machine shed to feather and gut the roosters. I watched Dad's face as he pulled them one by one from the crates. I could see no sign of aversion flash across his eyes, no hint of revulsion, as he raised the axe with his right arm and steadied his aim. How many times, I wondered, had he lifted an axe before he was able to kill a rooster without flinching?

When Marvin and I followed him into the pig house, we were careful not to disturb the sows lying beside their piglets, piled up like pink sausages. Dad slid his palm under one for Marvin and one for me, knowing we liked to snuggle their warm bodies against our chests.

Half a year after they were born, when they weighed more than two hundred pounds, a truck turned into our driveway. Marvin and I watched as Dad helped the men chase them up a ramp and into the back of the truck. The pigs squealed, bumping against each other, as the men turned their load out of our driveway.

"Where does the truck take them?" I once thought to ask Dad.

"We sell them for money—except for the one we keep for ourselves," he said. "That one gets turned into pork chops and put in our locker in town."

"Didn't you know that?" Marvin asked, chuckling as he looked at my stunned face.

But I had never thought about what happened to the pigs after the trucks turned out of our driveway. How could our father, who cradled piglets in his hands, chase them up a ramp to be hauled off to the St. Paul stockyards to be slaughtered?

Dad took pride in his work as a farmer. Each time he pointed his finger at President Garfield's signature on Homestead Certificate No. 4301, his weathered cheeks crumpled around the corners of his smile.

The ornate lettering—"pursuant to the Act of Congress approved 20th May, 1862"—documented the claim Ola Pettersson had made for eighty acres of the tallgrass prairie. The certificate was signed on

August 20, 1881, by President Garfield, seven weeks after he was shot by Charles J. Guiteau and four weeks before he died.

The ink in President Garfield's signature had faded, making it nearly impossible to decipher. Even so, Dad grinned with pride each time he pointed it out.

Our parents and their parents and the parents of their parents passed down a legacy of taking on responsibility at an early age and of enduring hardships with fortitude. Their way of thinking shaped Marvin's and my world. Was it the bondage of these beliefs, imposed on the oldest son, that powered my brother's psychotic terrors?

I clung to the father I loved, kind and gentle in his strength, secreting away in the far recesses of my mind an awareness of his capacity for cruelty and his capability to kill. But it bled into the sadness I brought to my therapy when I sat across the low, square table from Paul.

CHAPTER 21

I had become accustomed to the bright, primitive paintings that decorated the walls of Paul's waiting room as I cleared my thoughts of work and focused my mind on the things I had been mulling over since our last session. The hissing of the sound machine soothed me, as did the way Paul stepped back and smiled as he opened his door. After placing his pad of paper on his lap, he focused his gaze on me and waited for me to launch into a topic I wanted to discuss.

Over the course of the half year we'd been meeting, our sessions had fallen into a familiar pattern. I picked up a thread we had left hanging or launched into a new topic—an event from the past, a worry about a relationship, a letter I'd received from Mom.

Paul listened. He asked questions and nodded while watching my face.

The late-afternoon sun was casting a trapezoid of light across the wall as I pulled the box of tissues to within my reach. But instead of following our usual format, Paul astounded me with a question:

"Why don't you trust me?"

I had been stealing out of my office twice a week, before my workday ended, to walk down the long hallway. I had taken him back to the tics and the shrugs, the arguments in high school, the terror in my brother's eyes as his hallucinations gained control of his mind. Did he think all that I had revealed was superficial?

"It's hard for you to trust," he said.

I turned my head to break away from his gaze. Perhaps I had sounded too defensive, too protective of our family, but why would I denigrate my parents? Mom had done more for her children than any mother should have to do. Dad may have been harsh with Marvin at times, but he had good reason for his frustration. My brother could drive anyone crazy, always griping, never getting around to getting anything done.

"You've had your heart broken in three of your most important relationships—your high school boyfriend, your twin, and your mother."

I knew what it meant to have a broken heart, no longer wanting to get up and go to school because of a boyfriend. I was a teenager. Teenagers take everything too seriously. I learned a lesson, vowed to never again turn my heart over to someone else. A reasonable decision at the time. I'd been married for twenty-three years and had raised three children to their teenage years. Surely a heartbreak that long ago no longer had any significance.

And why did he include my twin? We had been close when we were small, spending all our time together with no other playmates around. But by the time we got to high school, I wondered if he would ever develop civilized manners, speak in coherent sentences instead of unintelligible grunts. Lots of sisters and brothers didn't get along, argued over trivial things. My heart wasn't broken. We simply drifted apart and had little to do with each other after he dropped out of Augsburg College—until his breakdown, which had landed me in Paul's office.

I had already told him the only feeling I had for Mom was a lack of feeling, a strange sense of numbness I couldn't explain—although her critical comments did bother me, the way she disapproved of my career and the way we raised our children. I had shown him one of her letters so he wouldn't think I was making it up.

Paul's eyes looked firm. Insistent.

"I think I've earned your trust."

I recoiled. All that nodding and smiling, his allowing me to pick the topics, letting me pace the conversation—had it been nothing more than a means of manipulating me in order to "earn my trust"?

"I need your trust in order for us to move forward with our work."

Had I known what the term "resistance" meant, I would not have realized it applied to me as I refused to consider any suggestions that I could construe as being critical of me or my parents. Even though I was unfamiliar with the concept, I understood what he was telling me—if I wanted him to be able to help me, I had to quit protecting myself and my family.

I had given him my mind, but he needed more. How could I trust him when I didn't trust myself? What if I grew to love him as he listened to me week after week while I poured out my sadness? I shrank into my chair and felt my neck flush as I confessed my fear of having my heart broken by him.

His expression softened. "Part of the process is to prepare for the ending," he said.

I moved to the couch.

The couch would serve to remove the social aspect of the therapy. It would allow us to go deeper, beneath the superficial.

I worried about my shoes. Coming directly from work, I arrived at the sessions in a suit and heels. Removing my shoes seemed unprofessional. Inappropriate. Still, my mother never allowed us to put our shoes on the sofa.

"Do whatever you wish," Paul said.

I removed my shoes and placed them on the floor. The pillow felt rigid against the back of my neck, my legs exposed. I tugged at my skirt, pulling it down until it covered my knees. I studied my feet. The spiral seams in my pantyhose and how they drew wavy lines across my toes. I stared at the wall. At the branches of a tree, visible through the small window at the side of the couch. What could be important enough for the couch? How would I be able to gauge Paul's reactions when I no longer could see his face?

I decided to continue by picking up a thread from a previous session—"I've been wondering…"—as if I was still sitting across the table from him. Whenever I stopped talking, he would say, "What are you thinking about?" in a voice so soft it sounded as if he feared he was interrupting some momentous thought. Sometimes I was thinking about the dreary color of the paint on the wall.

During one of our exchanges, he mentioned something he had suggested at several previous sessions. I fell into one of my long silences.

"What are you thinking about?"

"I'm trying it on."

"Thank you!" he said, his voice heavy with exasperation.

I wanted to smash his "thank you" in his face.

In a tightly written paragraph, buried in his responses to a series of questions on an insurance form, Paul had written:

> Early history in a strict fundamentalist religious tradition left her unprepared for the flexibility required of adult family life…

I had skipped over the comment, given it little credence. The reason I had gone into therapy was to ease my pain, not because I needed to become more flexible.

But the rigidity of my way of thinking was making our work difficult—my unwillingness to see how the heat of my reactions when my beliefs were challenged might be contributing to the tensions in my relationships, my inability to admit to any failings or changes I might need to make in how I responded to family and friends. No matter how complex an issue, I believed a stance was either right or wrong, that the world was made up of absolute good and absolute evil, that people were either saved or doomed. Even though I no longer espoused that dichotomy, I continued to view the world through a black-and-white lens.

As I lay on the couch, I began to think about things in my past. I had been hypercritical of my twin, superficial in my worries about what the popular kids thought. When Dad gave me more time to practice driving before our driver's tests, I had not been oblivious of his favoritism; I had put my needs ahead of what my brother also needed.

After several months, I found myself talking about our high school twentieth class reunion, the only reunion Marvin ever attended.

George and I had sat across a table from him and Sharon while dinner was being served. When the meal ended, our classmates gathered in groups to chat. I joined the cluster who had been my closest friends.

Marvin had worked himself into a nervous state. He would stride up to a group of classmates, interject a comment into the middle of their conversation, and before giving anyone a chance to respond, dash off.

I had watched the anguish in his face as he tried to break into one group, then another, and at his misery as Sharon gathered up their things and they fled from the room.

While I was describing my brother's agony, my throat became so tight I had difficulty finishing the story. "I could have helped him," I said, choking out the words. "I could have eased him into a conversation—but I was selfish—I wanted to talk to my friends."

My eyes smarted. My chest hurt. Unable to continue, I turned my face to the back of the sofa.

When Paul spoke, his voice sounded warm and gentle.

"Marilyn, being a twin has been a devastating experience for you."

Had he not been listening to all I had said? Did he not see I was the lucky twin, the twin who had gotten everything?

Still, the compassion in his voice flowed over me, like a cool summer rain on a parched field.

CHAPTER 22

Sharon's clear, plain script spilled over the two large sheets of notebook paper she had used to describe Marvin's diagnosis in a document she entitled, "A Synopsis of Marv's illness & our lives for last 8 mos." In September of 1987, she mailed copies to each member of their two families.

Her opening statement stunned me:

> Marv has a severe mental illness.

During his two-week stay in the psychiatric ward at the St. Paul-Ramsey Medical Center, he was diagnosed as having bipolar I disorder, also known as manic depression. Several months after his release, he stopped taking the prescribed medication because he refused to accept the diagnosis. "Lithium is for people who have manic depression," he said.

Six months after his breakdown at Mom's condominium, he suffered another psychotic break. This time, Sharon had to call the police.

After being admitted a second time to St. Paul-Ramsey, he refused to go back on lithium, which allowed Sharon and his doctors to witness the full extent of his illness. His psychiatrist prescribed two medications—Moban as an antipsychotic and Tegretol as an anticonvulsant—in place of the lithium.

At the end of the two overflowing pages, Sharon answered the question she had posed—"What does the future hold?"

> Marv can have more episodes, which would mean he
> is chronically mentally ill. He has no choice—to live

outside an institution, he has to take the drugs. His episodes are so bad, his disease prevents him from knowing how sick he is. His drugs cause side effects; it takes lots of dosage adjustment to get the amounts right. He is able to work now.

My chest tightened as I read her unsparing words. I felt as if I was sinking into a pit.

What had I not seen? What had I missed?

I had read his expressions as we built dams with the rain spilling over our faces, laughed with him as we lay across his bed with our favorite comic books, cried when he cried. His tics and shrugs had seemed to be nothing more than nervous habits, the way he showed his agitation. Lethargic and not wanting to get out of bed? Not uncommon among teenagers. Talked too loudly? Annoying, but merely a symptom of social awkwardness.

How much had I overlooked because I was unwilling to see that something wasn't right?

He had enlisted in the army in January 1964, but was unable to get a leave from his post in Germany for our wedding in November of that same year. The following summer, he spent several days with us in our apartment in Groton, Connecticut. I prepared his favorite foods—potatoes, pork chops, rice pudding—and mapped out a drive along the back roads to show off the countryside.

"This is what New England really looks like," I said. "Look at all the hills and the trees! Aren't they gorgeous?"

"Mmmm. They're nice," he said as he slid down in the seat and slept for the rest of our scenic ride. I wanted to kick him.

Not until he visited us on a second leave did I have more than fleeting misgivings about his mental stability. His long and vociferous argument with a telephone operator—"I'm trying to make a long-distance call! You're the one with a problem! You don't know what you're doing!"—disturbed me, but then he had always had a way of being persistent when trying to prove a point. The large array of plastic bags he had packed and his frenzy in carrying them seemed strange, yes, and yet I knew he became anxious when faced with a stressful situation like traveling from Germany to Connecticut and then on to Minnesota.

Instead of seeing his unusual behavior as a red flag, George and I chuckled at the things he did and said. But beneath my laughter, I was apprehensive. Something seemed not quite right with my brother.

He spent the remainder of that leave with our parents on the farm. In Mom's next letter, she gave no hint that anything had been amiss. I used her silence as justification to disregard my uneasiness, happy to go back to my life without having to worry about my brother.

In the fall of 1966, after Marvin had received an honorable discharge, George and I brought him with us on a weekend trip to Superior National Forest, a two-hour drive north of Duluth. Five months pregnant with our first child, I was relegated to sitting in the middle of the canoe, trolling for walleyes and northern pike, while Marvin sat on the seat in the front, my usual place.

"Can't you get a motor for this thing?" he said, as George and he dipped their paddles into the tranquil waters of Sawbill Lake.

"They forced us to sleep on the ground in the military—this is supposed to be fun?" he asked, as George drove metal spikes into the ground to secure our canvas tent on the wooded island where we camped.

"Can bears swim?" he wondered as he scanned the water between the island and the forest on the land surrounding it.

But in the evenings, he sat beside us on the boulders and listened to the call of the loons as pools of sunlight skated across the surface of the water. In those moments, he had seemed content.

Twenty years later, as I read the last sentence of Sharon's "Synopsis," I felt a heaviness infiltrate my body,

> We need your prayers and support for the unknown
> road ahead.

She made real the apprehension I had pushed aside. The manic behavior and the psychotic episode we had witnessed were not an anomaly.

My brother had a severe mental illness. It was not going to go away.

CHAPTER 23

I'm boiling apples and eggs in a kettle of water on a stove in the attic of our church.

"Would someone boil apples and eggs in the same kettle?" Paul asked.

The dream made no sense, I said. No one would do such a ridiculous thing.

Two tiny babies are flying off a Ferris wheel that is spinning out of control.

"Is that how your life feels?" he asked.

Marvin and I had watched the seats of the Ferris wheel dangle above our heads as we waited in line at the Kandiyohi County Fair. I clung to the bar on our bench while it lifted us into the night sky, my stomach swinging with the seat each time it lurched to a stop as the operator filled the seats below us. When we swayed back and forth at the top, my belly pressed against my chest. I had feared we would fly off into the immense empty space.

"Your brother had a breakdown everyone could see," Paul said. "You also are having a breakdown. But yours is an internal breakdown that no one can see."

Several weeks earlier, Paul had pointed at a hoop amidst a cluster of wall hangings. "The Native Americans call it a dream catcher," he said. "I'd like for you to try to remember your dreams. They might help us move forward in our work."

I stared at the webbed circle of wood, colored beads and feathers dangling from its side. It looked like something a tourist might have picked up at a roadside stand.

Marvin and I had been taught in our Sunday school classes that God used dreams to reveal his plans to the Old Testament prophets, who interpreted their own dreams as well as those of others. I had read about Buddha and his series of dreams that foretold his attainment of full enlightenment, and how Socrates looked to his dreams as a guide throughout his teaching career. I knew that Native Americans believed their dreams were sacred.

Even so, I considered the attempt to find meaning in a dream to be a form of hocus-pocus, like trying to extract someone's fortune from a glob of tea leaves lumped in the bottom of a cup, or predicting someone's future based on the way the sun moved through the signs of the zodiac two thousand years ago when my birthdate had moved from Scorpius to Virgo in the constellations as they appeared today.

I had stomached more than enough of "take by faith what you don't understand," of turning off your brain while sitting on a hard, wooden pew, of trying to boil apples and eggs in the same kettle.

Still, I had grown to trust Paul. I wondered what he might find in a dream.

My dreams eluded me. They refused to be caught in my net, disintegrating in front of the shade on our bedroom window the instant I tried to latch onto them. I placed a pad of paper beside our bed and pinned a dream down, recording it in the middle of the night. When my alarm went off, I found two tiny squiggles on the page.

One morning, before moving or opening my eyes, I snared a dream by running it back and forth, like a film, in my mind. I replayed it as I stepped into the shower and again as I steeped a cup of tea. The moment I sat down in my office, I wrote it down so I could bring it to Paul.

Soon I caught another. Then another. Not long after, I was inundated with dreams.

Paul received each one as if it was a gift—a precious jewel with multiple facets for us to examine. We followed the story the dream told, explored the images, examined the associations it brought to mind. They surfaced emotions I had repressed by pushing them out of my conscious mind. They exposed things I was too embarrassed to reveal.

"You talk yourself out of your feelings," Paul said. "Your dreams tell us what you feel."

It was as if my unconscious mind had decided to take part in the therapy, using my dreams as a portal to reveal what lay, hidden, beneath my rational thought. They opened a new reality for us to explore.

I am watching my brother Mark swim underwater in a glacial lake next to the garage on our farm as he slowly explores the cavities along the muddy sides. I'm terrified he cannot breathe, cannot survive in the subzero temperature of the clear, blue water. I watch in amazement as he pulls himself out of the lake, up onto the shore, and walks off, as if on his way to some destination.

"I think I know what the dream means!" I said, excited as I described it to Paul. "I'm both people. One part of me is unafraid, looking forward to exploring the murky spaces in my mind, but another part of me is terrified." He nodded, smiling as I went on. "I'm afraid of getting trapped in my unconscious—that it's a frigid, lifeless place where no one can survive."

I had seen what happened to my brother when he was imprisoned in his unconscious mind, unable to wake from his dreams. His glazed eyes remained vivid in my memory. Might I also get caught in the subzero water, where the rational self cannot survive?

"You have a strong mind," Paul said.

I have gone down to the basement of my childhood home. It is the middle of the night. I am distressed and want to see what is wrong, as my brother, five or six years old, is in the corner where Dad built a rudimentary bathroom.

I hear my brother making bleating cries, like a lost puppy or a lamb, but I am unable to see him. I am concerned about his immense sadness and distress. I fear he may have become permanently psychotic, that his cries are his recognition of his hopeless situation.

I go up to my parents' bedroom. My mother is awake, standing in their bedroom doorway. I ask her if she knows what is wrong with my brother. I ask if she has gone down to talk to him and comfort him. She too is distraught, but has done nothing, as she does not know what to do.

My father is asleep in their bed.

My heart was pounding, my forehead beaded with sweat, when I woke from the dream. I had heard my brother's cries—like a bleating lamb who had lost his way. Why had we been unable to rescue him?

Mom heard his distress but did not know what to do. "Is it something I did?" she asked her doctor. She read articles in the newspaper and in magazines as she struggled to understand his illness. She prayed for hours, asking God to heal him. Jesus cast out demons— why couldn't He cast out the demons that afflicted her son?

Dad lay, asleep, in their bed.

Before George and I visited Marvin at the St. Paul-Ramsey Medical Center, I had called to ask what we should and should not say. "Be open about his mental illness," a social worker had said. But I knew if we talked about a diagnosis he rejected, we would set him off on an angry tirade.

When we arrived, we found him slumped in a chair in the psychiatric unit. I wanted to take his arm, escort him out the door, drive him back to the farm. To go back to the beginning and start over. Do things differently.

His eyes radiated defiance as he glanced at us, his voice loud with agitation as we talked. He was angry at having been admitted for a third time to St. Paul-Ramsey.

"My actions would be considered normal—if I hadn't been branded with a label!"

He did not direct his words at me, but I knew he blamed me for his diagnosis, for his being seen as someone with a mental illness. I was the one who had overreacted by calling the police.

I felt sick when we had said goodbye and walked out the door. How had it come to this, I wondered, as we had driven out of the parking lot.

Paul looked stunned the day I refused the couch. I fixed him with a determined gaze.

"I'm finished," I said. "I'm not coming back."

I had made my decision to end the therapy several days earlier. My work with him obsessed me and was causing me to neglect my family and friends. Our youngest child, still in high school, needed my attention. It seemed our sessions would go on forever.

The work was very important, he said. We were making excellent progress. It was essential for me to continue the therapy. He coaxed, prodded, urged me to reconsider. As our session was about to end, I reluctantly agreed to return.

"You mentioned a dream you had this morning?" he said.

As our time was running out, I hurried through the dream.

I'm sitting on a hole in an ancient underground outhouse next to my ashen-faced father, who is staring straight ahead. He does not notice I am smearing my white nightgown with my feces as I try to wipe myself clean. I run up the steps that lead outside but am nearly naked in my soiled nightgown and have nowhere to go to escape.

On my drive home, I wondered why Paul had looked so distraught after I told him the dream. I did not realize it had revealed my unconscious reason for wanting to end the therapy. The revelations emerging as I lay on the couch were destroying the pristine image I held of myself, the means by which I validated my way of being. I felt naked, smeared with my own filth, humiliated as he sat behind me while I lay on the couch.

I had no place to run. No place to hide. More than once, I tried to escape the therapy.

My sister, Betty, tells me she wishes Mom and Dad would stop being silent about a family secret they have never spoken about. She says the secret is they had a son who drowned. I am surprised at her comment.

I realize I have vague knowledge of a brother who died. I tell her he died when he was twelve years old, that he was the same age as my twin and me. I tell her I am baffled that I cannot remember anything about him. He and I must have been very close and spent a lot of time together. I must have loved him very much. I too wish our parents would break their silence and tell us about our brother who died.

When I awaken, I am upset and want to immediately call my parents and ask about a brother who drowned. But I realize I am still asleep.

On Mondays, Marvin and I had ridden our tricycles in the basement as the Maytag washing machine gurgled and chugged while Mom thumped work shirts over her washboard with Fels-Naptha soap. "Move away," she said, overlapping the sheets and shirts while feeding them through the wringer. Water gushed out of the stream of clothes as it folded like ribbon candy into the metal washtubs. We chased each other between the sheets as they flapped and snapped in the wind, the can of clothespins screeching as Mom dragged it down the wire lines.

When she had fed the last load of overalls through the ringer, we begged her to lift the hose from the lip of the washing machine so we could hold our feet under the silky water and stomp in the whirlpool as it had gurgled down the drain.

Where had my love gone, I wondered, when the twin who stomped in the water with me slipped beneath the surface? Was the loss of the brother I loved so great it had to be locked away in the deep recesses of my unconscious mind, where only a dream could excavate it?

My mother is lying directly behind me, her body curved around my back, her arms circling my naked body. She slowly moves her hand over my breasts, strokes the soft skin on my abdomen, examines the lips of my vagina, slips the tip of her finger inside my anus and explores its perimeter.

Marvin and I had held our feet high to clear the cold porcelain sides as Mom lifted us into the claw-footed tub. We intertwined our legs, he at one end and I at the other, slapping them up and down to make a sea storm for our Ivory-soap boat.

"Don't play with your bellybuttons," Mom had cautioned.

Only later did I realize it had been her way of warning us of the sin of exploring our bodies, of the temptation of our sexuality.

I cringed when I told Paul the dream of my mother exploring my body, hurried through my embarrassment at the sexual imagery.

His voice was full of wonderment when he spoke.

"Marilyn. You are healing yourself."

CHAPTER 24

By the end of the third year, I wanted to be done, finished with the therapy. My sessions with Paul had become central to my existence. I needed to reconnect with my family and friends and to step back into my life outside of his office.

We had accomplished much. My inner barriers had collapsed as I poured out my sadness. And yet, despite years of work, we had not been able to find a way through the wall between my mother and me.

"You've been in a fight with her since you were born," Paul said. "Perhaps since before you were born."

I was unable to remember any incidents with Mom during the first years after Marvin and I were born, except one fragment—a time when she spanked us beside a large tree next to our church. But I couldn't remember what we had done wrong. I could think of no fights while we went to the one-room school. During our years in the town school, I didn't battle with her like Betty did. Marvin and I sneaked out to the movies, and I "forgot" to mention that we were learning to polka and waltz in the girls' phys ed class, hoping she would not hear about it from other parents in our church whose daughters sat on the bench while I waltzed around the gymnasium in the arms of another girl.

I had told Paul about the letter I wrote to Mom during my freshman year at Augsburg College. He had looked sad when I told him how I had ripped it up and burned the pieces after Mom mailed it back to me.

"*She lost a daughter*," he said. "*And you lost a mother.*"

I had never considered the impact the loss might have had on me—only the iciness of my retaliation as I incinerated the pieces of cream-colored stationary.

Getting at the source of my difficulty with Mom had never been a goal for me in the therapy. Paul's disappointment surprised me.

"Too deep," he said. "Too painful."

In his final updating of my treatment plan, required by my health insurance provider, Paul wrote:

> She has made excellent use of insight-oriented psychotherapy. Her self honesty and capacity for creative use of her mind [have] led to the uncovering of deeper layers of personality functioning and to a new liberation in the patient of a solid sense of self-esteem. Termination has begun…

At times, during the termination phase, I faltered, wondering if I had been too confident in my readiness to be finished with the therapy. I worried about my ability to continue my journey to self-understanding without Paul's guidance. He assured me I had become strong enough to continue the work on my own.

As our last session approached, I felt pumped up with a newfound joy. I dreamed I could fly. I gripped the books—*Dreams*, by Carl Gustav Jung, and *Dreamtime and Dreamwork: Decoding the Language of the Night*, edited by Stanley Krippner—that he handed me as a parting gift. On one of the title pages he wrote, "For Marilyn, and for the adventure and journey in dreaming."

I could find no words expansive enough to thank him for all he had done for me. In the security of his office, he had helped me come to grips with the reality of my past. I rediscovered the deep love I once had for my twin. Our work together had released me from the pain that had been weighing me down.

As I opened the door to step out of his office, he offered his final words of guidance:

"Look for your mother in your dreams."

CHAPTER 25

"Part of the process is to prepare for the ending," Paul had said. But how was I to have prepared for an ending without knowing the blow that ending would deliver? I thought I would bound back into my life, purged of the sources of my pain.

A week after I walked out of Paul's office, I basked in the ribbons of vermilion and ochre that streaked across the shoulders of the Berkshire hills as George drove me to the Hartford airport. My newfound exhilaration pumped me up during an assignment in Dayton, Ohio, where I assisted in the analysis of business plans for the various Mead divisions while sitting around a gleaming mahogany table on the eleventh floor of the downtown corporate offices.

When the six-week assignment ended, I returned to Lenox, still exuberant with my newly surfaced self-esteem as George and I awaited the return of our children—Naomi, working at the Chicago Northlight Theatre after graduating from the Rochester Institute of Technology; Nik, at Philips International after graduating from Wesleyan University in Connecticut; Stephanie, a sophomore at Yale—to spend the holidays with us.

It was after I had unpacked my suitcase that my euphoria evaporated. I plummeted into an ocean of grief. The void that Paul had filled with his compassion and caring felt immense.

As I descended into misery, my unconscious stepped in, inundating me with dreams.

I'm helping my twin clean his things out of his dormitory room, but as I wash them in the sink, the water overflows and floods the room. I realize the drainage pipes, deep in the ground, are blocked.

How many dreams did I have to dream about my brother? How far, how deep, had my anguish over my relationship with him pervaded my being?

My dreaming mind transported Paul to me, as vital as if I was sitting across the low square table from him. My grief made me feel excruciatingly alive and excruciatingly sad. My dreams served as lifeboats in a sea of loss. I clung to them.

A man who has been my lover for some time has told me he must go on to some other place. My anguish is immense. He has not and does not understand how deeply I have given myself to our relationship, as if it was only natural that he would move on.

I cry out as I take handfuls of jewels from a tray and scoop them into a bag, not caring I am giving him what was mine as well as his. I give him the bag of jewels so he can leave but continue to cry from deep in my soul.

It was as if the loss of my relationship with Paul had unleashed all my earlier losses. "Get up and get going" was the way I had avoided working through my grief, shoving my losses aside without comprehending the powerful grip the people I loved had held on my heart. As I walked through the woods near our house, the oranges and pinks of the descending sun escorted me—like the oranges and reds that lit up the wide horizon of the Minnesota sky. I thought of how far I had walked away from the world of our farm, of how much I had left behind.

My losses had been mounting. I could not contain them. The people I had taken for granted—my grandparents, long departed; my father, no longer alive.

Grandpa and Grandma Peterson had lived on the retirement place from the time Marvin and I were born until we left home, Grandpa working with Dad, Grandma bustling about in their kitchen. Marvin and I strolled down our driveway, across the gravel road, and down their driveway to visit Grandma when the men were working in the fields. The powdered dust in the tractor tracks felt like silk between my toes as we walked past the strawberry patch Grandpa had put in alongside their driveway, past the hollyhocks Grandma had planted on the side of the retirement house.

No matter how hard we slammed the door or how loudly we stomped up the steps in the entryway, Grandma threw up her arms in a fright when she saw us. We waited as she slipped her hand into the bodice of her housedress and rummaged through her petticoat to turn on her hearing aid, and as she adjusted the earphones, like pink peppermint candies, tucked into her ears. The heels of her lace-up shoes clicked as she walked into her pantry that smelled of cinnamon and cloves.

The shades in the windows clattered with the summer breeze as we drank tall glasses of milk and ate the rolled-out sugar cookies she had baked. She asked what Mom was doing, which fields the men were cultivating, if our brother, Mark, was taking a nap.

Three months before George and I were married, Grandma Peterson died of a stroke. "Pull yourself together" was how I had learned to deal with my heartaches. But pulling myself together did not erase the aching in my heart.

I had thought I could march ahead with my life, as if nothing had happened, after receiving Grandma's unspoken love for all those years.

And why had I thought I could so readily put Grandpa Peterson's death aside? As a child, I had seen him as an unsmiling but hard-working man whose hands shook with a tremor so strong the coffee splashed out of his cup.

He insisted on seeing the exact route the Augsburg College band was taking on our six-week concert tour to Alaska, the summer after my freshman year. He loved the idea of traveling but had taken little time to do so himself.

I marked our route on a large map of Canada and Alaska—up the Alcan Highway to Anchorage on two Jefferson buses; to Juneau, Sitka, and Ketchikan on a converted ice breaker; back to Minneapolis on the two buses—and hung it on the wall facing his bed. Each morning, after giving him a morphine injection to ease the pain of his cancer, Dad was to move a red tack to mark our progress along the route. "I'll send you lots of postcards," I told Grandpa, as I stuck a tack into Minneapolis, our point of departure.

He asked me to come and say goodbye before Mom and Dad drove me to Minneapolis. I walked down the same two driveways he had walked for more than twenty years to help Dad with the milking.

He had been waiting for me when I walked into the upstairs bedroom, where he now spent his days as well as his nights. He clasped my hand between his.

"I won't be here when you get back from Alaska."

When I had stepped onto the Jefferson bus that would take us to Alaska, David Wickman was standing alongside Mom and Dad as they waved while we drove away. We had become steadies again the summer before we started our freshman year at Augsburg College. I wore the ring he gave me, a black onyx stone embedded in a silver setting, on my left hand.

On the second day of our trip, one of his friends from their dormitory walked down the aisle of the bus and sat down beside me.

"Marilyn, there's something you need to know."

I slid the ring with the black onyx stone from my finger after he told me that David had been dating someone else at the same time as he was going steady with me.

The scenery—Peace River Valley, Steamboat Mountain, Indian Head Mountain, Summit Lake—passed by my window, like unsent postcards, as the Jefferson bus had headed north.

But the greatest loss was my father. I had never heard defeat in his calm, steady voice until I was thirty-eight and he was sixty-nine and he telephoned me from his room in the Rice Memorial Hospital in Willmar and asked me to come home.

His doctor agreed to release him so he could spend Father's Day with our family. We gathered around him in the retirement house and talked of the many things he had done that made us laugh—painted pink patches on the slate-colored walls of our living room, all the while refusing to acknowledge he was colorblind; cut off his eyelashes because they rubbed against the lenses of his glasses; stomped into the kitchen after evicting our pet duck from the henhouse and into the barn, saying, "That duck wouldn't let any of the hens drink when he was drinking! He wouldn't let them eat while he was eating! He yanked a feather out of the tail of every hen that walked by!"

When our day of remembering ended, he called us one by one into the bedroom where, no longer having the strength to sit, he lay on their bed. He told each of us what he admired about us and thanked us for the many good times we had shared.

A week later, when Mom and I no longer could care for him, she called the Kerkhoven rescue squad to transport him back to the hospital. He asked me to telephone their sisters and brothers and their spouses and ask them to come to the hospital so he could say goodbye. Too weak to hold a pen, he dictated a letter to his sister Jeanette, who lived in Florida, as he feared she would not have time to arrive before he died.

I stood at the side of the hospital bed when his doctor walked into the room.

"No more!" Dad said, his voice firm as he looked at the doctor.

A short time later the doctor returned, accompanied by a nurse from the clinic. A year earlier, I had watched her inject a long, fat cylinder of chemicals into Dad's vein. "I don't know how he does it," she said, after he stepped down from the examining table and thanked her. "He just stands up and walks out." My legs had wobbled as I followed him out the door.

With his nurse at his side, the doctor stood at the foot of the hospital bed, hands clasped in front of his white coat. He told Dad of the high regard the staff had for him, of their admiration of his fortitude and graciousness.

"It's been a privilege to be your doctor," he said.

Dad gripped the hands of each of the sisters and brothers and spouses as they leaned over his bed. "Give me a kiss," he said to Mom's sister Mildred. "Give me a kiss," to his sister Rose.

After the sisters and the brothers and their spouses departed, we stood beside his bed and held the hands that once held ours until his powerful heart could beat no more.

CHAPTER 26

*M*om had been lonely. Mark spent his days in the field. Sue was busy with her farmwife work and caring for their children. Even though Mom lived in the retirement house just across the road, she saw little of them. The nearest town was a seven-mile drive.

"I could die, and no one would know it," she wrote.

When she saw a newspaper article that described a new condominium building in Willmar, she arranged her finances and had left the farm behind. It was 1984, four years after Dad had died.

She began her days at 5:30 a.m. by delivering the newspapers, dropped inside the entrance, to each of the units in the building. She hosted prayer meetings and sewing groups in her living room. When her red 1984 Tempo needed to be cleaned, she washed it with a sponge and bucket of water in the basement parking garage. To get her exercise, she walked up and down the stairways between the floors for fifteen minutes each day.

As the years went by, she continued to write her weekly letters. I enjoyed her opening paragraphs, always with a description about the weather:

> It came in as a dull lamb; I hope it goes out as a shining lamb. I mean the month of March. I had an appointment at 9:00 a.m. At 5:00 a.m. it was soupy— thick soup—couldn't see the cars parked in the lot across the street. By 8:30 it was much better. The sun looked like the moon. So different. The temperature is in the early 30s. We aren't complaining.

Marvin had stopped responding to her letters after he kicked out the glass door to the building. He did not return her calls, nor did he visit her. She wrote "short letters, long letters, medium length letters, weekly letters, semiweekly letters" in her effort to reconnect with him. He met her barrage of words with silence. He and I included notes in our birthday and Christmas cards to each other, as well as sending an occasional letter.

A few months before Mom's eightieth birthday, I sent Marvin and Sharon an invitation to a party we were giving for her on June 6, 1994, at her condominium.

Marvin did not respond to the invitation. They did not come to the party.

Betty's face had turned an alarming shade of red as we dragged seventy-seven folding chairs up the steep slope to the back patio of the condominium building. Sweat streamed down my temples as we pulled another thirty chairs from a closet in the entertainment room and arranged them in rows in front of a speaker's stand. She buttered sixteen dozen buns for ham sandwiches while I blew up five bags of large balloons. Before we had time to float the lemon slices in the punchbowl, the guests began to arrive.

After the hour-long program ended, Mom circled through the clusters of guests, chatting with relatives and friends from the farm and introducing her new neighbors to members of her church. "I haven't even had a chance to eat any of my birthday cake," she said, as the last guest walked out the door and we began to fold up the chairs.

She had thoroughly enjoyed the party. All our hard work had been worthwhile.

Each day, on my drive home from Crane & Co., I stopped in front of the two rows of mailboxes mounted on a split-rail frame at the entrance to our street. The branches of five tall pine trees splayed their newly opened needles above me as I flipped through the mail— envelopes with cellophane windows; pamphlets filled with coupons;

announcements proclaiming, "You've been Pre-Approved!!"—while waiting for Mom's letter of thanks.

Two weeks after I had returned to Lenox, the letter arrived. I dropped my briefcase on our deck and leaned back in a lounge chair, taking in the warmth of the late afternoon sun as I slipped my index finger under the seal:

> June 19, 1994
>
> Dear George and Marilyn,
>
> Your name comes first, George, because this is Father's Day. This is the 13th year I have not enjoyed Father's Day. That is selfish I know, as I should say I enjoyed Father's Day 44 years with Winston as the father of the family we produced. The church service was special to the fathers and the feeling "within" was special. Without a father, there can't be a family…

I had no interest in her discourse on the importance of fathers and Father's Day. I wanted to know what she had thought about the party. I found her comments on page three:

> Now, a different subject—my birthday, June 6th, 1994, was a busy day in unit 202 in Regency Condo—but the busiest section was on [the] main floor—the entertainment room and kitchen! We were busy! Had you (George) been here, you would have taken care of the sound system, carrying chairs, blowing up balloons, greeting guests, and pouring punch….

Betty and I were the ones who lugged the chairs. We set up the sound system and fought with the microphone. And I had done a whole lot more—planned the event, arranged the program, prepared my notes as MC—beginning the planning an entire year ahead of the party. Why was she crediting George with what he "would have done" when he hadn't been able to join me on the trip?

I swatted my hair out of my face and read on:

> I was <u>so</u> happy to see <u>Mark,</u> but not for long, as he
> was showered with many very important duties so he
> disappeared from my sight.

Mark had "many very important duties"? He had been busy with
fieldwork, walking in half an hour *after* the first guests arrived, while
Betty and I dashed back and forth brewing pots of coffee, refilling the
punch bowl, and greeting the guests.

> I answered a Gladys Wareburg question that she
> asked me, "Don't you think you are expecting too
> much of your daughters?" My answer: "I think they
> are expecting too much of their mom!" Later I real-
> ized she was serious—I tho't she was joking.

I shot out of my chair and paced back and forth. She had watched
Betty and me as we ran up and down the stairways carrying boxes and
bags from multiple trips to the stores. She saw us race back and forth
while spreading tablecloths on the tables and arranging platters of
ham before dashing to our bedroom to change into our party clothes
when the first guests began to arrive. Even her neighbor had recognized how hard we were working!

> You know, George, I have all the years given Marilyn,
> Marvin, and Mark high honors for never being
> scolded for keeping late (early?) hours. Thank good-
> ness I gave my two daughters a condo key and a #202
> key—I don't let anyone in at 1:30 a.m. So at the age
> of 52 years and 9 months and ? days and hours—
> Marilyn broke her honorable record! I guess I'll leave
> the scolding my daughter deserved to you, George.

I froze in my footsteps. She wanted George to scold me for staying out late when I was out with friends at a high school reunion,
some of whom I hadn't seen for thirty-five years? What made her

think she was entitled to stand as a judge over me? That my husband had the right to tell me what to do?

Scribbled in a side margin on the last page, I found the "thank you" I had been looking for:

P.S. THANX for everything!!!!!

I flung the letter into the bottom drawer of our desk and kicked the drawer shut.

Two months later, I had cooled off enough to pick up the phone. I dialed her number on a Sunday afternoon, the time I had always called, allowing her to finish her nap after returning from church. We fell into our familiar pattern. I listened and asked questions while she talked about her luncheons, her visits with Mark, the work she did with the Widows/Widowers Friendship Group.

A year earlier, when I told her I was leaving Mead to take a position as the manager of a new venture at Crane & Co., she did not respond. When I told her about my preparations for a three-week business trip to Hong Kong and Tokyo, she had said, "But who is going to cook for George?"

I decided to run a test. For the next several weeks, I volunteered nothing about my family or me or my work and noted how much time had gone by before she noticed our conversations had been only about her. On my third call, after talking for an hour, we had yet to move past a discussion of her activities.

"Mom, I've got to stop talking. It's time to fix dinner."

"Before you hang up, tell me about George and your children."

"They're fine," I said, and slammed the receiver into the cradle.

After all my hard work with Paul, I was taken aback at the intensity of my rage. I had no idea that, beneath my lack of feeling for my mother, I still cared so much.

CHAPTER 27

During two of our trips to Minnesota, George and I had driven to the St. Paul-Ramsey Medical Center to visit Marvin. I had begun to suspect that his being in a psychiatric ward when we arrived was not a coincidence—that telling him about our visits two or three months ahead of time was serving as a trigger for him to stop taking his medications, leaving enough time for his mood to accelerate into mania and a psychotic break.

Like many with bipolar disorder, he may have stopped taking his medications because he wanted to prove he didn't need them, thereby indicating he did not have a mental illness. He may have craved the high of mania as a means of gearing up for the stress of spending time with our extended family. Perhaps he wanted to be free of the side effects. At times, I wondered if he was acting out an unconscious desire to disrupt our family gatherings.

Instead of giving him several months of warning, I decided to wait until three or four days before our arrival. "Marvin, we're flying in on Wednesday morning," I would say. "How about we meet for lunch at Applebee's?"

In June of 1995, we found him waiting on a bench inside the entry at Applebee's—a chain of family-friendly restaurants. He always arrived before George and I did. I greeted him with a hug, his body as unyielding as a slab of granite. Like the rest of our relatives, he greeted people, even his twin, with a firm handshake.

He hunched his shoulders up and down, shoved his fork back and forth, and created deep furrows in his forehead as he lifted and lowered his eyebrows. It was as if I had been dropped back into high school and was sitting across from him at the old kitchen table. He fiddled with his glasses while telling George about his latest duct-tape fix to the rearview mirror of his car, which he called his "vehicle." The sharp pitch of his laugh made me shrink. I wanted to shave off his bristly beard, trim the clumps of blond hair that straggled over the back of his collar, tell him to take off the pounds that puffed out his belly.

I asked about Sharon's work as a software programmer at Lutheran Brotherhood; how their daughter, Kristi, one of the top five in her class of five hundred, was doing in school; and about her synchronized and competitive swimming teams. We told him about Naomi, working at the Goodman Theatre in Chicago; Nik, on a graduate degree in computer science at Columbia University; and Stephanie in her second year of a PhD program in neuroscience at Brown.

"So, what do you do at Cub?" I asked.

"Whatever they ask me to do. Sometimes I stock shelves. I'm trying to get more hours."

He had held on to his job assembling circuit boards as an electronics technician at Control Data, despite repeated hospitalizations. But six years after his breakdown at Mom's condominium, the company had merged two of its divisions. He was among the two hundred people who were laid off.

Two years after the layoff, unable to find another position in the field of electronics, he had taken a part-time, entry-level job at a nearby Cub Foods grocery store. He wanted more hours, but Sharon had told us he had as many as he could handle. His manager had warned him to stay on his medications if he wanted to keep his job.

By then, Tegretol was affecting his liver. His psychiatrist had switched him to Depakote, but the medication had proved to be less effective at controlling his moods.

As George drove out of the Applebee's parking lot, I slid down in the seat of our rental car and watched the towns scattered along US Highway 12 pass by my window on the two-hour drive to Mom's condominium.

Our visits at Applebee's no longer satisfied me. I had little opportunity to talk to my twin, and yet I allowed myself to be put off by something as superficial as his appearance. We wasted the time we had by talking about mundane things. By the time we left Applebee's, I felt more alienated from my brother than when he greeted us at the entry.

Four months after our visit, with our fifty-fourth birthday approaching, I sat down to write my usual update of news to include with my card to Marvin—George's new career teaching physics and chemistry to middle school students, after taking early retirement from General Electric; my traveling in a new position as manager of sales and marketing for currency papers at Crane & Co.

But before I started to write, I considered the things I wanted to discuss with my brother. My early connection with him had a profound and lasting influence on all my subsequent relationships. Why did I settle for skimming along the surface instead of trying to understand the unique nature of the ties we once shared?

As was true of most twins, we had received a lot of attention. I hid behind Mom's skirt when people said, "They look so much alike!" As we grew older, I tried to respond to their questions—"What is it like to be a twin?"—although I had no means of knowing what life would be like without a twin.

People tended to see two babies born at the same time as an oddity, as if they were two halves of a whole. Some of the ancient peoples believed twins had different fathers, one conceived by a spirit, either evil or divine, the other by a mortal human being—a "good twin" and an "evil twin." Some cultures honored twins; some worshipped them. Others feared or defamed them. One twin might be abandoned and left to die in the elements or be buried alive in a clay pot. Both twins as well as their mother might be sacrificed—unless the father was fond of his wife and offered up a female slave in her place.

In recent times, psychologists had been more concerned about the psychological impact of being a twin on the twins themselves and how it affected their development. Twins have several tendencies in common. Because two infants begin their lives vying for the attention of one mother, they tend to become highly competitive.

The Old Testament twins, Esau and Jacob, were intense rivals. When Esau returned, faint with hunger, from his work as a hunter, Jacob talked him into giving up his birthright as the firstborn son for a bowl of lentil stew. Jacob colluded with Rebekah, their mother, to trick Isaac, their blind and aged father, into giving him the blessing that rightfully belonged to Esau.

But success in a fierce rivalry between twins is often tainted by powerful and conflicting emotions:

> And Esau hated Jacob because of the blessing where-
> with his father blessed him: and Esau said in his heart,
> "The days of mourning for my father are at hand;
> then will I slay my brother Jacob." (Genesis 27:41)

My competitive nature became apparent when Marvin and I stepped into the one-room school. I battled with David Smith to be first in line, to reach the sum of a column on the blackboard before he did. In high school, I practiced long hours to hold the position of first chair, first trombone; I studied diligently each evening in order to become the valedictorian. But like other twins, I felt conflicted by my successes, as if I had taken the whole portion when half should have gone to Marvin.

Psychologists worry about the intense bonding that occurs between twins, that they risk seeing their twin not as a separate person but as a part of their own self, that they might include their twin inside their own self-boundary. To reduce this danger, twins need to be treated as separate and different individuals. Our parents knew nothing of this concern. They referred to us as a single unit—"the twins." Mom enjoyed dressing us in matching clothes. I enjoyed wearing them.

Each twin needs to be free to develop at his or her own pace. When compared to the other twin, one may feel of less value for being "behind" and the other guilty for being "ahead," both ending up with psychological baggage. Mom didn't think Marvin was ready to start first grade. Even so, she had driven us to the one-room school at the same time.

Knowing the close linkages between twins, I worried about my chances of developing bipolar disorder. "Mom, is it going to happen to you?" our children had asked, eyes wide with fright, after witnessing Marvin's breakdown in Mom's condominium.

Because Marvin and I are fraternal twins, we share half of the same genes, the same proportion as is shared between non-twin siblings; my risk of developing bipolar disorder is no greater than Betty's or Mark's. Even so, our chance is slightly higher than in the general population because someone in our family has the disorder.

A number of studies indicate that bipolar disorder is caused by the abnormal functioning of the brain circuits that regulate mood, energy, and thinking, as well as our biological rhythms. Still, the illness is not driven by genetics alone. If one of a pair of identical twins—who share all the same genes—has the illness, the other twin does not always develop it. A combination of genetic factors and environmental triggers—stress, trauma, intense emotional conflicts in families—are believed to be involved. Given that Marvin had a genetic propensity to develop the illness, I wondered if his struggle with Dad and the conflicts and stresses it created in his life acted as a trigger for his developing the illness.

Shortly after the Minnesota Family Twin Study was begun in 1983, the researchers contacted both Marvin and me in their goal to include all the twins born in the state between 1936 and 1955 in the analysis. Their objective was to assess the genetic and environmental influences on a variety of physical and psychological characteristics.

I knew that twins—identical twins raised together, identical twins raised apart, nonidentical twins raised together, nonidentical twins raised apart—were ideal research subjects because of their genetic linkages and shared childhoods.

I willingly filled out the long surveys. Marvin refused to participate.

"Twins supposedly have a lot of problems," he had said, his voice filled with disdain. "I don't want to get involved in any of that."

CHAPTER 28

I chose not to mention the Minnesota Family Twin Study in the letter I enclosed with my card to Marvin for our fifty-fourth birthday. I did, however, write about the psychological risks surrounding twins and how I thought we might have been impacted by them. I also told him I had spent more than three years in therapy. It was the first time I had mentioned it to him.

Each evening, I stepped onto the mat of pine needles in front of the row of mailboxes, like farmers' domed lunch buckets, as I waited for his response. His penmanship—some letters charging forward, some tilting back, all climbing in an upward trajectory—immediately caught my eye.

Without taking the time to remove my coat, I pulled from the envelope a disappointingly small sheet of notepaper, the same size as the ones he usually filled with trivia.

But this time, he had filled both sides:

Wed, Nov 8, 1995

Dear Marilyn,

I am writing this in the bathtub, so I hope I don't drop it. I am on my feet for my shift except for 1 ten minute break, so I do this to revitalize the old body.

Interesting letter! I guess I did not know your feelings regarding the past. My hindsight is Mark was Dad's favorite & I was Mom's favorite. That left you & Betty more to fend for yourselves emotionally.

I think Mom is trying to compensate now, especially to Betty.

My only regrets are we were encouraged to lie about our whereabouts & Betty & I about our smoking. I also had no control over bedwetting, which can traumatize anyone drastically & drive an emotional wedge between family members. Mom had sheets, etc. to wash extra & Dad was downright cruel—I suppose out of utter frustration with me.

Chester was my 2nd father & Kenton a good role model—luckily! Dad, being a typical Scandinavian, was not one to say "I love you" or "You did good," which I had to find elsewhere. However, on his deathbed he said I had the best marriage???

This should be enough information for you to digest for now!

Love,
Marv

The words "I was Mom's favorite" leaped off the page. She had threatened, "From now on, I'm not waking you!" She had commanded, "Before you do anything else, you're going to sit down and put in a half hour on your clarinet!" And yet, despite her insistent harassing, he had perceived her favoritism.

I had spent more than thirty-five years feeling guilty for having benefited from Dad's partiality. At the same time, Marvin knew he was being favored by Mom. How many of the Old Testament twin themes had our family played out?

And Isaac loved Esau…but Rebekah loved Jacob.
(Genesis 25:28)

Marvin had never spoken of his bedwetting. I was stunned that he had written about it. Dad had fumed as he dragged him out of bed. Buzzers screeched. Alarm clocks clanged. The anguish of his words—"traumatize," "downright cruel," "emotional wedge"—cried out from his letter.

We had spent all our time together. We had read each other's faces. We knew each other's fears. And yet, the stigma of bedwetting had prevented him from talking about his suffering.

I had not known of his close attachment to our uncle Kenton, Mom's brother who had married Dad's sister Rose. But I was not surprised. Kenton had a gentle disposition, always treating us with kindness the many summers Marvin and I had spent long days playing with their children, Jerry and Margaret.

Nor did I know of the important role Chester had played in his life. Dad had given up his education at the West Central School of Agriculture to help care for Chester, who, at the age of six, had become severely ill with diabetes. Dad treated him with compassion and respect, even though he remained dependent on their parents and lived with them his entire life. If Dad had been aware of the impact of depression on an adolescent, had he understood Marvin's mental illness, might he have had the same compassion for him as he had for Chester?

Chester was forty-one when he died from the toll of diabetes. Marvin was twenty-one when he lost his second father—the father who took him fishing.

I had written pages about the impact of two infants sharing one uterus, two children caught up in a complex dynamic of family alliances, two destinies tangled together because of a random biological event. Marvin did not mention any of these issues.

Paul once said, "Being a twin has been a devastating experience for you." At the time, I thought he had turned the reality upside down. Now I wondered—had being a twin been more painful for me than it had been for Marvin?

For the first time—the only time—Marvin and I had shared our perspectives as we looked back at the undercurrents in our family. He had revealed a glimpse of how he experienced our childhood. The bonds that joined us together still existed, in spite of me being put off by his tics and shrugs, of our decades of sketchy communications, of my having called the police.

His perception of the past changed my reality. He had let me see our family through his eyes.

I considered whether I might also be able to mend my relationship with my mother by writing to her from my heart, as I had done with Marvin. I wanted to be able to speak freely and to be authentic in what I thought and felt.

With her eighty-second birthday approaching, I sat down to write a letter to enclose with my card. But as I picked up my pen, I found that bitterness does not readily release its claws. The words she had written thirty-three years earlier flashed through my mind:

> I've treasured this letter and kept it in a special place,
> but I no longer want it. You are <u>not</u> the daughter I
> thought you were!!

I wondered where that "special place" might have been. Perhaps she had slipped my letter under her stack of embroidered handkerchiefs in the chest of drawers she shared with Dad. She might have tucked it into a box with her other treasured letters, sliding it onto the shelf above the housedresses hanging on her side of their closet.

Why did she return the letter I had filled with my love? She may have thought I had become arrogant after graduating summa cum laude from Augsburg College. Still, she understood ambition and had wanted to go on to normal school and become a teacher. "I think she's jealous of you," Betty once said. But why would a mother resent a daughter's accomplishments? Perhaps she sensed my disdain for a woman settling to be "no more" than a housewife, that the pride I took in my accomplishments discredited her life.

She may have assumed I had turned my back on living a Christian life when Sharon and I put the top down on her black Falcon and drove off to California. Our departure for six weeks of fun could have caused her to stomp into their bedroom and grab my letter from under her stack of handkerchiefs because she felt betrayed that I no longer walked in her footsteps. My stepping out of her control might have been the reason she washed her hands of me. The Bible said that disciples of Christ must put their faith above everything, even above their children:

> If any man come to me, and hate not his father, and mother, and wife, and children, and brethren, and sisters, yea, and his own life also, he cannot be my disciple. (Luke 14:26)

For decades, I had cushioned myself behind a numbness that allowed me to detach myself from her. It was time for me to let go of my long-held vengeance over a returned letter.

Once again, I filled pages telling her of my many happy memories and my love for her. By going back, I hoped to repair that rupture and begin again. We could go down a different path—a path that would lead us back to that special place.

A grapevine spiraled down the split-rail fence as I pulled Mom's response from our mailbox. I tossed my briefcase on the kitchen table and extracted three sheets of tablet paper from the envelope. In her usual manner, she had filled both sides of each sheet with the long, slanted loops of her script.

I hurried through the details about the health problems of one of Dad's cousins; the arrangements Betty had made for the two of them to fly to Lenox for our daughter Naomi's wedding; the contents of a note she had received from Marvin, who, after a decade of stonewalling her, had begun to respond to her volley of letters. Six pages of news, but not one word about the letter I had written to her.

Thinking she might not have received my letter before she wrote hers, I lifted our phone from its carrier.

"Mom, the letter I wrote—the one I sent you for your birthday—did you get it?"

"Yes, I got it."

"Did you like what I wrote?"

"Oh yes. It was similar to the letters I already got from two of my other children. When I get letter number four, my collection will be complete."

Had I not staggered from the blow to my heart, I might have tried to take into account her perspective, that she had no way of knowing the long and arduous journey that had brought me to this place. I might have tried to consider her obliviousness of my longing for her to champion me, to give me her blessing. I might have realized that she did not know how much I wanted her to validate me by approving of me and my life. But my wounded soul overpowered my capacity to see it through her eyes.

I had deluded myself into thinking a letter, even one filled with love and praise, would elicit a thoughtful and loving response. I had blown myself up with the same old fantasy.

CHAPTER 29

I had never shouted at my mother. Not when I was a child and stood at the head of the basement stairway and she, on the landing halfway down, scolded me for something I had not done; instead of defending myself, I clamped my teeth together and remained silent. I did not shout at her when she said we were not allowed to play Whist because the game used "playing cards," the same as were used for gambling; that cards could be sinful when no one was placing bets made no sense to me. I felt left out when my friends dealt their hands in Jack's Café, but I did not stand up to her. When we returned from an hour of Sunday school, followed by a one-and-a-half-hour morning worship service, and she refused to give me permission to knit because knitting was "work," and we were not allowed to work on Sunday, I complained. I asked how something done for pleasure could be considered work, but I never sassed her. I did not challenge her when she said medical school would be too hard or when she reminded me I was the daughter of a dirt farmer or when she said I should stay home with our children instead of going back to school for my MBA.

I did not stand up to her until late September of 1997, three days after George and I had returned from the funeral for Betty's husband, Dale, and I opened our mailbox and found her letter. She had to have written it the same day as George and I had boarded a plane to return to Lenox.

The letter was short, two pages instead of her usual six. She had omitted an opening paragraph about the weather:

I don't know if I ever explained this to you. I will now.

When she had to "explain" something to me, I knew she was angry. I fortified myself.

> I decided Stephanie's wedding would be a good time for Marv and Mark to do something together. Then you called (or wrote) and told me he should not be encouraged to be at the wedding and you asked me to write to him saying he should come at a time when there would be less people. Much as I disliked to do this, I did the letter. I never knew how he accepted the suggestion. I only knew he wasn't there.

We had settled the issue—or so I had thought—of her pressuring Marvin to come to Lenox for our daughter Stephanie's wedding. Flying to Massachusetts to mingle at dinners and parties with people he didn't know would have put him under a high level of stress. I feared he would go off his medications and arrive in a manic state, and as his mania accelerated, he'd disrupt the festivities—and if worse came to worse, he might end up in a psychiatric unit at the Berkshire Medical Center.

I had asked her to stop insisting he go to the wedding, telling her it would be better for him to come at a less stressful time.

> Don't ever ask me to write a letter of that type again. It took me a long time to make it "kind." I won't be the "in-between" guy—as it really hurt me. When I wrote to him thinking he would go and enjoy going, I knew he had the invitation. An invitation is an invitation. I didn't think I had done anything wrong. He has finally gotten friendly with me again, and I intend to keep it that way.

Something deep within me erupted. She was the one who had tried to appropriate Stephanie's wedding for her own purposes—without a thought about the impact it might have on Stephanie or me or anyone else who happened to be around. She knew what could happen. She had witnessed the chaos his breakdown brought about in her condominium. She had left it to George and me to manage the crisis, to call the police, to get him the medical care he needed.

Now that Marvin had "gotten friendly" after a decade of stonewalling her, she had turned on me. She had made me into his adversary.

I stomped into the kitchen and yanked the phone from its cradle.

"I just got home and read your letter," I said, my voice shaking with rage. "I can't believe what you've written. I can't believe you're blaming me for Marvin and the wedding. You know full well why I didn't think it was smart for him to come! You know full well he ends up in the hospital when he gets stressed out!"

"Well he was fine at Dale's funeral. He was just as normal as the rest of us."

"You may have thought he was fine," I said, screaming the words into the phone. "What about all those times when he wasn't fine? What about all those times he's ended up in the psychiatric ward? Why couldn't you let *him* decide if he could handle the wedding?"

"He had an invitation. An invitation is an invitation," she said, sounding smug. "Why did you invite him if you didn't want him to come?"

I wanted to smash the phone in her face. I had tried to protect Stephanie and my family as well as myself from having to deal with a manic episode during a wedding, as well as to protect Marvin from her stress-invoking demand that he go to an event he did not want to attend.

"I didn't say I didn't want him to come. I asked you to stop *pressuring* him to come!"

"Well I thought it would be a good time for him to be part of the family, and he could be with Mark. I knew Mark would take care of him—"

"Did you ever think that Mark might not want to spend his time worrying about Marvin? Mark had never been to our house. Why didn't you think about asking him *before* you started pressuring Marvin?"

"Well, I had it all figured out. Marvin and Mark could sleep in Naomi's bedroom, Betty could sleep on the sofa bed in the basement—"

"The wedding wasn't about Marvin—it was about Stephanie! Why does everything have to be about him?"

"Well, I feel sorry for Marvin. I want him to be included. I've finally won him back. It really hurt me when you made me tell him he couldn't come—"

"I didn't say he couldn't come. I told you to *stop pressuring him!*"

"Well, you said—"

"*I didn't do it! I'm not responsible for what happened! Don't blame me for something that wasn't my fault!*"

I had responded to the corrective "sermons" she mailed to me by defending myself in a return letter—until I realized my defensive replies reinforced her use of a pen as a weapon. She waited until she had returned from a meeting where someone said something of which she disapproved, a family gathering where someone did something she disliked, or until George and I had departed for the airport, before picking up her pen. While in the heat of her rage, she wrote a letter reprimanding the person who had sparked her wrath. She stuffed the letter into the mailbox, slammed the lid shut, and marched back to the house. She never had to cringe at the pain in the eyes of the recipient. Never had to witness the wounds inflicted by her pen.

I switched to retaliating with silence, hoping she would become worried that she had offended me and think twice before sending another reprimanding letter. But she continued her letters, undeterred by my lack of response.

As my anger cooled, I began to think about all her hard work and the many good things she had done. After several weeks, I felt remorseful for cutting her off. I resumed my letters and telephone calls as if nothing had happened.

At the end of one of my sessions with Paul, I had mentioned a letter I had just received from Mom.

"Would it hurt her if once—just once—she could say something nice?" I said, my voice breaking as I stood up from the couch.

"How can you do that? Push away what you feel?" he had asked, shaking his head as I took a deep breath and prepared to walk out the door.

But I had a lifetime of experience in pulling back my anger, in never revealing my hurt, in burying my pain. Marvin had also locked up his anger and packed it away where no one could see it—until the day he obliterated his restraints in a psychotic rage. Only then, after seeing his rampaging mind, had I felt a need to go back and examine the undertow beneath our way of life.

A week after I shouted at Mom, I had calmed myself enough to call my sister. We relied on each other if we needed a sympathetic ear. When she received a nasty letter from Mom, I stood up for her; when I received one, she stood up for me. I used her as my reality check, to tell me if I was justified in what I felt.

She had always treated me, her little sister, with patience and generosity over the years. She taught me how to thrust my arm back and forth—"*Go, Eagles, go!*"—while swinging pompoms on our lawn. I walked proudly down the hallway of the town school in the navy-blue skirt and jacket with a red-and-white-striped blouse that she sewed for me, identical to the outfit she had sewn for herself. When I needed a ride after a game, she had let me ride in the backseat as her boyfriend drove her home.

"I've had enough of it!" she said, after I described the way I had yelled at Mom, her voice bristling as I stared at the stark branches of the maple trees that pierced the dreary October sky.

"What have you had enough of?" I said, taken aback by the rage in her voice.

"Nothing you do is right! You can't please her!"

"I don't get it—what is it I do that's so terrible?"

"It's everything. You're hard to live with. You serve strange food. You expect too much of your children. You send them to schools that are too hard. You're always showing Marvin up. On and on. It never stops!"

A squirrel clamored up a branch and leaped to another tree as I paused to take in what Betty had said. "Did she have anything to say about my shouting at her?" I asked. "I've never shouted at her before. Didn't that slow her down?"

"Nothing has changed. She just grumbled, 'Marilyn doesn't always have to think she's so perfect.'"

The squirrel scrambled down the tree trunk and disappeared into the woods as Betty waited for a response that I was too exhausted to give.

I felt depleted. Drained of vitality.

When Betty continued, her voice had lost its strident tone. "You do so much for her—way more than the rest of us—and she doesn't appreciate any of it. I just wish it wasn't so important to you."

How can a mother's love not be important? How can a daughter stop longing for a mother's affirmation, for wanting her blessing? I had tried to escape from her disparaging words by leaping to a new branch, by hiding in the woods, by crawling under my bed.

"Maybe it's because she's so worried about Marvin," I said. "Maybe it's because she can't think about anything else—"

"Marilyn. Nothing has changed. She's ridiculed everything you do for as long as I can remember—since way before Marvin got sick. I'm tired of listening to it."

CHAPTER 30

As we turned off US Highway 12 and headed north, the corn swayed in glistening waves as far as we could see, the rows so tightly planted no spaces could be seen. The farmers sprayed their fields with herbicides so they didn't need space between the rows. I remembered when Dad planted our corn with his four-row corn planter. He pulled his cultivator down and across the rows to gouge out the weeds, the spaces between the rows—lengthwise, crosswise, diagonal—remaining visible as the corn grew. He thought sixty-five bushels of corn per acre was a fine harvest. Now the farmers reaped two hundred bushels per acre. Sometimes more.

We passed long rows of cylinder-shaped bales of hay encased in white plastic, like giant vacuum-cleaner hoses stretched across the fields. Each bale was so heavy, it had to be lifted by a tractor fit with special equipment. Dad had baled rectangular bales with his baler, each one light enough for a farmer to carry.

Our rental car kicked up a plume of dust as we turned onto the gravel road going west. I remembered how Marvin and I had steered our bicycles within the smooth tire tracks to avoid skidding on the pebbles when we pedaled to Kandiyohi County School District No. 54. The school no longer pointed a long, slender finger into the sky. It had closed a few years after our brother, Mark, completed the six grades. Someone hauled it twelve miles away and recycled it into a house. Another of the one-room schools was lugged by a neighbor into his barnyard. He spread straw over the varnished hardwood floor and used it to house his pigs.

When Ola Pettersson homesteaded eighty acres, one square mile of land encompassed four or more farms. His farm, now owned by my brother Mark, had been expanded to 633 acres, just under one square mile, with three of the four farmers long gone. His farm was considered small. Many of the neighboring farmers, working with their sons, had increased the land they owned to a thousand acres. Some worked four or five thousand acres by renting land from other farmers. One was said to farm thirty-five thousand acres—fifty-five square miles—working land scattered across farms all the way into the Dakotas.

"Look. There are cows grazing in our pasture. Mark must be renting it out," I said, as we approached his driveway.

Dad's dozen Holsteins had grazed their way to the far end of the pasture and back again, arriving at the gate in time for the evening milking. A mile away, a neighbor and his sons had expanded their dairy operation to 350 cows. One of our cousins and his sons, living a few miles in the opposite direction, owned a thousand cows. Not far from Kerkhoven, a corporate farm had more than eight thousand in its herd.

Dad had sold our cows by the time Mark had earned a BS in plant and soil sciences at the University of Minnesota and returned to take over the farm. He had also gotten rid of the chickens.

Each year, Mark raised 750 pigs of a choice breed and sold them into a specialty market. Some of the operators who sold into the commodity market produced more than twelve thousand pigs a year.

When I stepped out of the car, I took in the breadth of the wide sky and the fertile scent of the earth. I listened to the stillness of the flat land. It was as if I was standing in the footsteps of my parents, of my grandparents, of my great-grandparents, as if I was surrounded by switch grass and Indian grass and orange coneflowers.

But in the spring of 1998, for the first time in the thirty-nine years since I graduated from high school, I did not want to return.

I had written to Paul, telling him how I had shouted at Mom.

"Your suppressed rage showed itself for a bit," he wrote in return.

If the power of what I had felt represented a "bit" of my suppressed rage, I wondered what might happen if the full force of my wrath escaped.

Still, it had been more than a half year since my explosion, and Mom was begging us to come. I remembered how the crowing of the roosters had awakened me, the way the morning light warmed the prairie sky, and decided to return.

Mom's voice was loud enough for me to hear as she clinked dishes in her kitchen while I sat on the sofa in the living room of her condominium. I realized she was talking to me.

"You talk too much!" she said. "Marvin and I can't get a word in edgewise when you're around!"

The *Kerkhoven Banner* fell to my lap.

"I told him he should come and visit while you're here, but by the time you stop talking, I've forgotten what I want to say! Marvin and I are quiet people."

Mom thought of herself as a quiet person? I had listened to her chat with her sisters, Mildred or Elsie or Gladyce, on a sizzling August afternoon while the men were working in the fields. They sat at our kitchen table sipping coffee while discussing their nieces and nephews, their neighbors, the minister's wife. The sun had dropped low in the west by the time the sister said it was time to hurry home and fix supper. She was eager to discuss the details of my conversations as soon as I walked in the door when I returned from a visit with a friend while home from college, relishing every tidbit of news I brought back from an afternoon with a classmate or cousin.

While it was true Marvin tended to have little to say, when he got going, he talked as much as anyone, continuing with his favorite topic after everyone else had veered off in a new direction. During his manic episodes, he became belligerent, his voice drowning out anyone who tried to speak.

"I haven't heard back from him," she said, clanking plates as she piled them into the cabinet. "If he comes tomorrow—I told him he should come in time for our noon meal—you need to give him a chance to talk!"

I whacked the *Banner* onto the coffee table.

"At Betty's house, after Dale's funeral, he had a photograph he wanted to show you, but he didn't have a chance because *you* were so busy talking."

I strode down the hallway and slammed the door to our bedroom. I gripped the armrests of the rocking chair and pressed my head against the back of the headrest while telling myself to get my rage under control.

I remembered hearing the same words two decades earlier, when George and I and our young children spent the holiday visiting Mom and Dad in the retirement house. The entire family had crowded around the extended table for our Thanksgiving meal. After a long day of working in the kitchen, Mom dropped dollops of whipped cream onto slices of her homemade pumpkin pie and passed them around the table. Her face lit up as she launched into a story about one of our neighbors.

Dad listened for a minute. "Be quiet!" he said, his voice sharp with annoyance. "You talk too much!"

Everyone turned to Dad. But I watched Mom, the color fading from her cheeks as she slumped in her chair. I had wanted to put my arms around her.

With my hands clamped on the arms of the rocking chair, I considered how I might respond after she had made the same accusation of me. If I was somewhere else while Marvin was present, she would not be able to accuse me of preventing him from talking.

I strode into the kitchen. "Since you haven't heard anything from Marvin, I assume he's not coming," I said, pulling the telephone directory from a drawer. "I'm calling Mary to see if I can spend the afternoon with her."

Without letting Mom know he was coming, Marvin arrived in time for the noontime meal. I said nothing while we ate. When Mom brought out the dessert, I told him I had thought he wasn't able to come so had made other plans. I walked out the door.

By the time I returned from my visit with Mary, Marvin had departed. I steeped a cup of tea and sat down at the table. Mom poured a cup of coffee and sat down across from me.

"Marvin and I had a very good visit," she said. "He had lots to say, and I listened to every word."

When I heard the smug satisfaction in her voice, I realized she was pleased I had departed for the afternoon. She wanted Marvin to herself. She had used me as her bait—as a means of enticing Marvin to visit her.

"How is Mary?" she asked, as she sipped her coffee. "I haven't had a chance to catch up with her lately. What all did she have to say?"

"She's fine."

"Did she say anything about Ardell and Katie? I hear they have two more grandchildren on the way, both due this summer—one in July, I think."

"She didn't mention them."

"Did you see Harry? Was he out working? Did she say anything about them getting the crops in? It's been a wet spring—"

"No."

I picked up the *West Central Tribune* and turned to the editorial page.

She could find out how much she enjoyed having me around when I didn't talk too much. When I didn't say anything at all.

CHAPTER 31

My apprehension had been justified. My simmering cauldron had threatened to boil over during our visit with Mom. When we returned to Lenox, I ended my weekly calls and stopped writing. I became the quiet one.

Unabated by my silence, she continued to write her letters.

My silence served as a pretense, a cover, as I seethed with rage. After weeks of venting, I withdrew to a place deep within and tried to discern the source of my anger.

As if to assist me, my unconscious stepped in with a barrage of dreams—I'm climbing a spire that extends high into a radiant, crystal-clear sky. I'm terrified as I inch my way up the rungs of the ladder, unable to make my way into the lookout tower at the top. I'm able to see two small figures:

> A kneeling man and woman chiseled out of ordinary wood, lying on the floor of the tower. I think they might be Mary and Joseph, or Adam and Eve, or representations of some ancient religious beliefs. I am too frightened to ascend any further, but what I have seen is enough.

I tried to think of the questions Paul might have asked: What was going on in my life that felt like a long, lonely, terrifying search? Was I seeking a comprehensive understanding of all the issues, while overlooking something quite ordinary that would tell me all I needed to know? Did the revelation I was seeking reside within two roughly hewn religious figures? What ancient religious beliefs might the figures represent?

> Wives, submit yourselves unto your own husbands, as unto the Lord.
>
> For the husband is the head of the wife, even as Christ is the head of the church: and he is the saviour of the body.
>
> Therefore as the church is subject unto Christ, so let the wives be to their own husbands in every thing. (Ephesians 5: 22–24)

George and I believed a husband and wife were to be equal partners as we led, protected, and provided for our children. By the time he took early retirement from General Electric, I earned an income equal to his. When I departed on business trips, he took full responsibility for the children. He unloaded the dishwasher and tossed clothes into the washer and dryer as often as I did. I rejected my parents' belief that a woman should be deferential to her husband. Was that the reason for Mom's animosity?

Might it have something to do with their views on the rights, the authority, and the responsibilities of the firstborn son—another ancient theme woven throughout the Bible?

Like Esau, Marvin had given up his "birthright," allowing all that came with it to pass on to his younger brother:

> And Esau said, Behold, I am at the point to die: and what profit shall this birthright do to me?
>
> And Jacob said, Swear to me this day; and he sware unto him: and he sold his birthright unto Jacob. (Genesis 25: 32–33)

Perhaps Mom resented my lifestyle. Tycoons in Lenox were constructing mansions with as many as one hundred rooms while settlers in the tallgrass prairie were building dugouts and sod houses. But I did not live in a mansion, and she did not live in a dugout.

Maybe she felt I was arrogant because she had worked as a house-keeper and I hired a housekeeper to clean our house. "I guess money grows on trees in Lenox," she once said to Betty. But George and I had shoehorned evening courses into our schedules to earn graduate degrees while our children were young, studying long hours after they went to bed. We juggled our work and travel schedules so one of us would be at home with them in the evenings. Why would a mother begrudge a daughter the successes she had worked so hard to achieve?

My dream told me that "*what I have seen is enough*," but I did not understand the revelation it contained. The insight I sought involved a man and a woman who represented ancient religious beliefs. My intuition told me it also had something to do with being a twin.

I continued my regime of silence for two months after our visit with Mom. At the same time, I struggled to rid myself of my yearning for her love and support and for her to end her criticism of me and my life.

Still, I was unable to stop myself from another attempt to break through our stalemate. I wrote another letter.

The needles hung like ragged feathers from the branches of the pines as I pulled her response, mailed on September 15, 1998, from our mailbox. She went on for pages with excuses:

> I remember very well watching Marvin waiting to say something at Betty's…I went to get a second piece of pizza when he came to me and said, "I wanted to show a picture, but no, I didn't get a chance." He didn't ask for an answer, but walked out to the car shed and looked at cars. I watched him and intended to talk to him. Marvin gets hurt feelings easily. Winston and I learned that. I don't know if he even had hurt feelings this time—he only said one sentence or two to me.

It had been a long day. Betty had invited her family and friends to her home after the interment for her husband. I sat next to Sharon in the crowded living room, as she had told me she had two photo albums she wanted to show me. George and Marvin stood behind us, chatting while Sharon turned the pages in the albums. A tangle of noisy conversations separated us from Mom, sitting on a sofa across the room from us.

"Here is Kristi with Bluey," Sharon said as she pointed at Kristi's cat.

"This one we took when we were visiting her at Luther College," she said, directing me to the next page.

After we had looked at the photographs, I hurried to the kitchen to help set out the hot dishes and salads Betty's friends had dropped off for the reception. Her daughter Cindy and I took the dog for a walk so we would have a few minutes to talk; I'd rarely had a chance to see her after she had moved to California seventeen years earlier. When we returned, Marvin and Sharon had departed.

Why did Mom obsess over a single comment Marvin made as he passed by her chair? She could have shown her concern for her daughter who had lost a husband, or she might have spent the time chatting with her granddaughters.

I shook my head as I continued to read her letter. I had written that I wanted her to be interested in my children; she wrote that she did not tell anyone what my children did because her "memory does not do well when it comes to complicated school studies." I had said I wanted her to take an interest in my career; she said that she told people which countries I traveled to, but then hastened to add, "Ask me no more—and I'll tell you no lies." I wondered what lies she might have told.

> I always will give you credit for helping to get Marvin
> to the school bus on time.

Was that the only thing she had seen? Was that all she knew of my attachment to my twin?

> I really have only Mark to talk to if I have any family problems. He told me he couldn't see any significance in problems. If someone hurts his feelings, he thinks it best to skip it and forget about it. I told him it was good advice and I have tried to keep it.
>
> So if you can forgive, please try to do so. I think some of the stuff you are remembering should be old enough to dispose of. I have no pets as you seem to think. I have thought of you all as very good to each other and certainly to me. I want it that way.
>
> For every bad memory—there is a good memory. Look for it—you'll find it.

I remembered the way she steadied my head as she coaxed me to drink the orange juice she had just squeezed when I had pneumonia and my fever rose to 104.5, the way I tried to take a sip or two to please her. I remembered how she hurried into the bedroom when I screamed that there were spiders crawling between the sheets, how I huddled in a chair as she stripped the sheets from the bed, the cool, clean touch of the fresh ones. I remembered how I shivered as she swathed an icy towel across my forehead, my body shaking with chills as she changed my sweat-soaked pajamas, the pillows she fluffed in our platform rocker, her propping them around me, how she pushed the rocker into the doorway to the kitchen so I could be with the family while they ate, and how, after a short time, I asked to be carried back to bed so I could return to the respite of sleep. I remembered the way her face had slipped in and out of my fever-laden dreams.

Five decades after the hallucinations of my childhood fevers, a daughter, chubby and innocent, sometimes as an infant, sometimes as a toddler, began to occupy my dreams. I'm consumed by terror when I suddenly remember that I have a daughter whom I've forgotten. I run down a steep stairway or hurry into a bedroom to rescue her. I find her in an infant seat or in a cradle at the bottom of the staircase or lying on a bed in a bedroom. Always, she is silently waiting for me to return. Always, she is waiting for me to remember her.

What memory was my unconscious mind transporting to my conscious mind with this recurring dream? Again, I went back to comb through our history. This time, I searched for a daughter who might have been ill, a child who might have died, an infant no longer remembered. I read the family stories Mom had written, searched through old photographs, studied the genealogy searches put together by our relatives. It did not take long to discover the many deaths in the life of Mom's father.

After Hjalmar and Maria had moved into an upstairs bedroom in our house, Mom heard him say again and again, "She's yust like Emma!" as he watched Marvin and me at play. When I brought my report cards home from our one-room school, he would say, "She's so much like Emma!"

Mom asked her father to tell her about the Emma he was remembering. He told her the story of his half sister.

When Mom learned about Emma's death and the grief her father had suffered, she had become terrified. Like Emma, I was pale and suffered from lung congestions—colds, bronchitis, pneumonia. Like Emma, I might die.

After Mom told me the story, I asked her why she had never mentioned Emma.

"I didn't want to frighten you."

She had wanted to shield me from her terror. But when I was burning with a fever, I had felt the tenderness of her care. I had sensed her compassion and the depth of her concern.

At my next annual visit with Paul, I told him about Hjalmar's many losses. We discussed the way trauma is passed down from generation to generation.

"Could my grandfather's loss of Emma—someone he loved so much—could his grief have been passed down to my mother?" I asked. "And through Mom, in some kind of mysterious way, could that loss have been passed down to me? Might Emma be the forgotten daughter in my recurring dream?"

CHAPTER 32

*M*arvin responded immediately to the letter I had included with the card I sent him for our fifty-seventh birthday:

10/29/98

Dear Marilyn,

Kristi just went back yesterday* so I intentionally am late with your card. Actually this is good as I can answer your letter which came today.

My car is really good—air conditioner doesn't leak, power lock is repaired, "wood" panels stayed on (George & I glued them) & mileage is terrific as well as get up & go!

As far as the photo album goes I think Mom exaggerated—I too talk when I should be listening at times, but I have tried really hard to not pass this on to Kristi. I also have changed the subject to something more to my liking (boredom) at times which is really rude!

Anyhow our children learn from our faults or the lack thereof—that's how I see it—I am glad you are seeing the thumbs up fruits of your labor now! We are all good—was nice to see you (other than a funeral visit) as Mom would say & congratulations on upcoming grandparenting!

Last night was choir practice & I am regretting coming out of retirement. The director called me up & the pastor also asked me to come back. I tried to tell her I am losing the top end of my range.

Betty does not call me so I am not up to date until Mom writes. I had been calling often after Dale's death.

Love as always,
Marv

* semester break

The letter contained more information than his usual scanty reporting of their news. I treasured the new openness and warmth I sensed in our relationship. Mom had tried to form an alliance with him, pitting him against me, but he didn't see it that way.

Even so, I heard reproach in his statement, "I too talk when I should be listening." His comment gave credence to her accusation.

I cowered before breaking the seal of Mom's letters. Her rebuttals battered my sense of self-worth. What drove me to continue our destructive exchange? Her accusations—I was critical of others and always had to be right; I was arrogant and proud of my career, violating the biblical admonition "Pride goeth before destruction, and an haughty spirit before a fall"—caused me to descend into a pit of self-recrimination and despair.

I felt alone. As if I had been cast aside.

My broken sleep wore me down, depleting me of the resilience I needed in my new position as manager of strategic initiatives at Crane & Co. To break my pattern of lying awake in the middle of the night, my doctor prescribed Ambien.

After a month of dreamless nights, I found my dreams to be more vital to my wellbeing than unbroken sleep. I did not understand how neurons generated dreams, passing impulses from one synapse to another, but they served as a guide in my search for what had gone wrong between my mother and me. "Look for your mother in your dreams," Paul had said when we ended the therapy.

As I fell into despair, she began to appear in my dreams:

My mother and I are sitting together in the back row of a chapel filled with people. I notice my father is sitting two-thirds of the way to the front. I wonder how this can be possible, since he has died and been prepared for burial. Something miraculous has happened. I think how people will become excited as they discern his presence. I see reporters with cameras, who will soon be taking his photograph.

He stands and walks to the aisle, turns, and looks directly at me. He calls my name and holds his arms wide to embrace me. I think how both my mother and I should go to him to celebrate this profound event. But he is only calling me. I feel sad for my mother but am overcome with joy as I run to his arms.

We hold each other in a tight embrace as we turn in a circle of joy. Tears stream down my face. Cameras flash in our faces as the reporters record, for the world to see, how much my father loves and treasures me.

I had been strong as we helped my father through his final days, standing beside his hospital bed as he made clear by squeezing our hands that, although he no longer could speak, he was listening to our conversations. I had remained serene as the minister intoned the words "and to dust you shall return" while our relatives and friends stood beneath the vast blue sky that arched over the cemetery behind the Salem Evangelical Covenant Church. I remembered how Dad had loved that sky and the fertile earth beneath it. When George and I, on our way to the airport, stood beside the black soil mounded over his grave, I did not yet feel the extent of my loss.

His death did not become real until six weeks after his last breath. It was then I began to cry and could not stop.

"Why don't you check and see if there's anything in my toolbox," Dad would say, his neck lined with sweat and grime as he carried his lunch bucket up the three concrete steps of the entry into our house.

I raced to his tractor, knowing from his grin what I would find. After lifting the cover of the metal tool case on the side of the engine, hot from an afternoon of cutting alfalfa, I peered into its shady recesses. There I found the small cottontail—old enough to be on its own but not big enough to hop faster than Dad could run—huddled between the pliers and wrenches.

With its warm body tucked under my shirt, I carried it to a patch of clover next to the granary, where I ran my fingers through the clumps of down behind its ears, stroked the fur on its long hind feet, and fluffed its puffy little tail. It wiggled its tiny nose as it nibbled the sprigs of clover I held in front of its mouth.

When Mom stepped out on the porch and shouted, "Supper is ready!" I carried the baby rabbit across the gravel road. After stroking its back and kissing it between its ears one last time, I released it in a patch of weeds.

I knew it was meant to be free. And I knew Dad would catch more baby rabbits for me.

My dream had brought my father back to me, as vital as if he was still alive. After fortifying myself in his steady, unspoken love, I pulled myself out of my despair. I decided to stand my ground with Mom by writing another letter.

She stood her ground as well:

> I hope you can forgive—only then can you be for-given. I can forgive and forget—not much of a prob-lem. We could talk about fun things and forget the dumb subjects. So please forget the past. Let's live our lives as if we are enjoying living. It costs little. Then I can be happy again.
>
> Love, Mom

P.S. If this isn't good enough—skip it! It's good enough for me—

It was good enough for her. But it was not good enough for me.

CHAPTER 33

I went down into our basement to search for old family photographs. On one of the shelves, I came across a small white box with a narrow pink stripe that bordered the cover. Mom had turned the "Baby Dear" book over to me some years earlier, but I had set it aside and forgotten about it. I wondered what I might find behind its pink padded satin cover, embossed with a sprig of apple blossoms.

I flipped through the sixteen pages in the small book. Two of them contained a list of the gifts we had received at the time of our birth:

> Mr. & Mrs. Chester Magnuson and family—75¢ and a cake.
>
> Emma Bengtson—50¢
>
> Mr. & Mrs. Walfred Gustafson—powder, soap, and a cake
>
> Mr. & Mrs. Leanard Halvorson—woolen socks, garters...

I remembered garters—the elastic suspenders stretched from my shoulders to my thighs as they held up my long stockings under the dresses I wore in our one-room school. No matter how I laid them out on my bed, they twisted and tangled as I pulled them over my head. The rubber discs pinched my fingers when I wedged them into the metal clips. The brown cotton stockings made my legs itch.

On warm days, I hid in the cloak hall and rolled the stockings down around my ankles, but the clips slapped against my skin when

Gayle and I raced out the door for recess. I had begged Mom to let me wear a garter belt that fit around my hips, like the older girls wore.

I turned to the page where Mom listed our Christmas gifts and noted the ones we had received the year we turned three:

> Little wagons from Grandma & Grandpa Peterson
> Horsie to ride on from Mother & Daddy
> Rubber dolls from Grandma & Grandpa Johnson…

Dad had built the "horsie" in his workshop, with strands of twine as a mane and a hunk of frayed rope as a tail. He painted the rough wood with white house paint, adding several large black spots. Marvin and I slapped the leather reins against the horsie's neck and rocked it so fast it lurched across our wooden floors.

He built the rocking horse because there were no toys in the stores. Six weeks after we were born, Mom had called their Sunday afternoon guests—her parents, her mother's sister Lottie, her sister Gladyce and her family—into the kitchen. "Something serious has happened!" she said, as they crowded around the radio to hear the announcement that had interrupted the program. The Japanese navy had bombed the US naval base in Pearl Harbor.

Marvin and I knew nothing of the war. We were oblivious of the shortages. Dad built toys from scraps of wood in his workshop, and Mom made teddy bears from old fur coats. She sewed our clothes and recycled my dresses and his shirts and pants with our cousins.

Having two babies qualified our household for two additional ration books, giving her more coupons than she needed. She used them to buy coffee and sugar cubes as special Christmas gifts for her parents. When the war ended, she sewed matching sailor suits for Marvin and me from the WAVES uniform Dad's sister Jeanette had worn.

When the stores were able to restock their shelves, Mom bought toys—Tinkertoys, Lincoln Logs, dominos, metal spinning tops—and gave Marvin and me identical gifts for Christmas as well as for our birthdays. But the year we turned nine, she gave Marvin an Erector Set and me a life-sized "Magic Skin" doll with clothes—dress, bonnet, wedding gown, and veil—that she had sewn for it. I did not want a doll; I wanted an Erector Set like the one she gave Marvin. A few weeks after Christmas, I wrapped the doll in a blanket and asked Dad to carry it up the ladder that led to our attic. I told Mom I was saving it for the daughter I would have some day.

What I did not know was that she had given me the doll to prepare me for the baby she was expecting in a few months. When our brother Mark was a year old, I dressed him in the wedding gown and veil. Mom had laughed as hard as the rest of us as he walked across the room carrying a bouquet of paper flowers.

I turned to the page with spaces for recording my height for each of our first seven years. She had made no entries after the first year. On the page with spaces for my weight, the entries ended the year I turned two. Three of the pages had no entries at all.

On the "Baby Was Named" page, she had added a few comments:

> To name a pair of twins was not the easiest. Mother thought of many names but Daddy already wanted his boy "<u>Marvin</u>" so we matched up Marilyn with it. This is easily pronounced and easily remembered.

The phrase, "easily pronounced and easily remembered," sounded like something Dad would have said. The words reflected his manner of speech, his way of thinking. Of the many names Mom suggested, did she like the one "they" had selected?

I turned to "Baby's First Word":

> Marilyn and Marvin were slow to talk. Seemed as if they could understand each other without talking. They said "Mama" to whomever they talked to.

Neither of us had learned how to talk, as we were left to entertain each other while she went about her work. With little chance to hear adult language, we learned to communicate by reading expressions, watching actions, and taking in the other's moods.

Even so, I was surprised at how old I was before I could patch together a couple of words:

> "Open door, see chickie, see chickie!" came from Marilyn when she was 2 ½ years when daddy had brought home 300 little chickens and mother and daddy thought the "twins" could watch from the windows but Marilyn was far from satisfied until she got in and helped throw the chickens out of the boxes.

Each spring, Marvin and I had waited for Dad, driving our 1938 Ford, to return from the P. A. Miller Hatchery in Kerkhoven. We ran behind him as he carried a dozen large cardboard boxes from the car into the brooder house where we poked our fingers into the round air holes on the sides of the cartons, laughing as the chicks pecked our fingers with their tiny beaks. After cupping our hands around a tiny ball of yellow fluff, we released it near the oil-burning stove in the center of the small, square building.

We stood beside Mom as she filled the little troughs with chick feed and watched as she poured water into their glass watering jars. Large bubbles gurgled to the top as she flipped them over and the water flowed into the saucers. The chicks dipped their beaks into the saucers and tipped their heads back, the water trickling down their throats.

And Mom had thought I'd be satisfied to watch all of that through a window?

On the "Baby Walks" page, she had also added a bit of description:

> Little Marilyn walked across the room two weeks before she had her first birthday, but the little girl was so very careless she had some bumps—didn't walk again until a week over a year [after her birthday] and still wasn't careful, so stayed in her walker.

Marilyn didn't get to real walking until fourteen months, but then she and Marvin really walked and were careful too so didn't get many bumps.

The phrase "so very careless" struck me as peculiar. How would a toddler learn to walk if she wasn't "careless" enough to risk falling? The words "so stayed in her walker" also seemed odd. I had seen the small, square, black-and-white photographs she took of Marvin and me in the clunky, secondhand metal walkers with large metal trays jutting out in front of the wooden handlebars.

A toddler who could walk across a room would not have chosen to "stay" in a contraption that cumbersome. She had to have kept me in it even though I was able to walk.

I waited until Sunday afternoon, my usual time to call, before punching the speed-dial number I had programmed for Mom. To avoid triggering her defenses, I chatted a bit before asking my questions.

"You know, Mom, there's something I've been meaning to ask you. I've never been able to remember much of anything from when I was small—except for one time. You spanked Marvin and me next to a big tree beside our church. Do you have any idea what it is I'm remembering?"

"I'm shocked you remember it. You were so little. You couldn't have been more than two or three."

"But I don't have any idea what we did—why did you spank us?"

"Oh, I remember it all right," she said, her voice relaxing into the story. "It was during a Sunday morning service. You and Marvin started to laugh. No matter what I did, I couldn't get the two of you to quit it. So I took both of you outside and spanked you. It was on the north side of the church. There used to be a big tree there. After that, you sat quietly during the services. I still can't believe you remember it!"

"I have another question. You wrote in my baby book that Marvin and I were slow to talk. Why did it take so long for us to say anything?"

"Well, clearly, you didn't get enough attention."

Her response astounded me. Instead of her usual defensiveness, she stated it as if it was a known fact.

"And Mom, I just found my baby book. You wrote that I walked across the room when I was eleven months old. Do you remember it?"

"Oh yes, I remember it well."

"You said that I was 'careless.' I don't know what you mean by that."

"You didn't hold on to anything. You just walked across the room."

"But Mom, here's the part I don't get—if I was able to walk all the way across a room, why did you keep me in my walker for three more months?"

She hesitated for a long time before replying.

"I guess you waited for Marvin."

Not long after our conversation, I again dreamed my recurring dream about my forgotten daughter. I rush down a stairway and find her lying in a baby carrier next to the bottom step. Again, she has been silently waiting for me to remember her, to return to retrieve her. Again, I pick her up and hold her tightly to my chest.

But this time, I speak to her:

> *"It's all right to be angry," I say. "It's a terrible thing I have done to you."*
>
> *She does not respond, so I repeat my words. "It's all right to be angry. It's a terrible thing I have done to you."*
>
> *But she continues to cry. I realize she is much too young, too innocent, and too dependent to be capable of feeling anger.*

CHAPTER 34

I was going to have to drag it out of Betty. She knew something I wanted to know. Her email had arrived just as I was getting ready to log off my computer and end my workday. After rushing through the long tirade, I stared at her final diatribe:

> [I]t just upset me so much he [Marvin] can get six pages of pats on the back for absolutely no reason and you, who do[es] EVERYTHING FOR HER, GET NOTHING!

What had Mom written that caused Betty to explode in a deluge of capital letters? The minute I walked into our kitchen, I called her.

"She doesn't have any problem sending our letters to whomever she pleases," I said, begging her to tell me what Mom had said. "So why are you so worried about sending one of her letters to me?"

Betty, too, was fed up with Mom and her critical comments. I realized that her own reservoir of anger might be the fuel firing her rage on my behalf. I had seen her lash out at Mom when she claimed that Adam and Eve wore leather skirts. "Mom, that's ridiculous!" she said. "Where on earth did you hear that? Adam and Eve were naked!"

"I don't care if you make fun of me," Mom had said, huffing her indignation. "I believe it because it's true!"

How could I convince Betty to let me see Mom's letter?

I pleaded. She resisted.

"I'd send the letter to you. I really would like to, but there are some lines in it I don't want you to see." She thought for a moment. "I suppose I could blacken those lines out—"

"Don't blacken anything out! I'm sick of being in the dark. I want to know what's really going on—I want the truth!"

Five days later, I skimmed down the many pages Mom had written to Betty. I scanned through the paragraphs, searching for the lines she had wanted to blacken out.

She hadn't exaggerated. Mom had gone on and on—"It was the best day I have had for a long long time!"—about Marvin's visit, page after page of singing his praises. He had proclaimed his love for Betty and her daughters and had "shed tears" for their kindness. He described his love of Mark and Sue and their children. "Everyone he talked about he loved." She extolled his every action. "He also got down on the floor and cleaned under my refrig. Then he looked at my dishwasher and found something there to fix. He was a perfect man all day."

I shook my head, wondering why neither she nor Betty had recognized the symptoms of mania—his nonstop chattering, his emotional outpouring, the way he jumped from one activity to another.

Instead of being alarmed, Mom had found his flood of words to be energizing, causing her to pour out her emotions as well:

> I love your daughters, Jeanne and Cindy, and their children. I really love Cindy's husband. George has always been so good to me. Marilyn was very nice this trip.

A few weeks before Mom wrote the letter, she had flown to Lenox to spend the holiday week with us. We had enjoyed her visit. She relaxed in the loveseat while she watched George and me lay on our bellies beside our Christmas tree, fitting triangles and stars into a blue plastic ball with our nine-month-old granddaughter, Clara. Nik sat beside her, tracing his finger from tractors to pigs to the windmill in a photo album as they talked about our many visits to the farm. George kept her cup filled—"a little cream, but no sugar"—with steaming coffee, while Naomi propped pillows behind her back. She chuckled as Stephanie flipped large rounds of lefse on our lefse grill with the turner Dad had sanded down from a wooden yardstick.

At the age of eighty-six, her flesh hung in loose folds from her arms as she sipped her coffee. The skin on her face had crumpled into deep wrinkles. Webs of blue blood vessels marked the backs of her hands. Her white hair retained no hint of the red she had detested. When I walked her up the stairway to her bedroom and kissed her goodnight, the creases in her cheek had felt soft against my lips.

We had always catered to her as if she was a queen. Why did she limit my kind and thoughtful treatment of her to "this trip"?

> Sue has told me at least two different times she likes
> Marvin. She has never talked about Marilyn.

Why did she need to insinuate that Mark's wife, Sue, didn't like me? Did she believe that for someone to like Marvin, that person had to dislike me?

Each time George and I traveled to Minnesota, Mark and Sue invited us to the farm for a meal. We relaxed around their kitchen table for hours while Mark and I chatted about our memories of growing up on the farm. Sue took part in our conversations. I valued her insights, her "outside" view of the complex relationships in our family.

> I can't help myself from thinking Marilyn should
> remember to love Marvin a bit more.

I bolted out of my chair and stomped across the room. How dared she assess the amount of love I had for my twin! Who gave her the right to act as a judge over what I felt?

I know he wasn't [at] their wedding. I don't know if
he was invited.

"Has she lost her *fricking* mind?" I shouted at the empty kitchen.
She *knew* Marvin had been sent to Germany early in the year George
and I were married. She *knew* he had been unable to get a leave to be
the best man in our wedding. She *knew* I had asked our double cousin
Jerry to stand in for him.

I think more of Marvin than I think of Marilyn—
because she thinks so much of herself.

I froze as I read the words. I stood in silence as I read them again.
As I read them yet another time.
"*So that is what you think.*" The letter drooped in my hand. "*That
is what you think of me.*"

The February days shrouded the Berkshire hills in a dank fog as
I grappled with the words Mom had written as I struggled to come
to terms with what I no longer could escape. How does a daughter
accept a revelation that slashes through her heart?
I had been clinging to a delusion, pursuing a fantasy I could not
attain. It was time to face the reality:

My mother loved my twin. She did not love me.

When Betty realized how deeply I had been hurt, she apologized
again and again for letting me read Mom's letter. But I was grateful.
She had given me what I needed. What I sensed, she had made concrete. Now I could pin Mom down.
A month after I received the letter from Betty, I felt ready to
punch the speed-dial number. I skipped my usual niceties.
"You said I didn't invite Marvin to our wedding," I said, my voice
sounding as weary as I felt. "Don't you remember he was supposed
to be our best man? Don't you remember he was in Germany and
couldn't get a leave?"

"I guess I forgot that."

"Well, Mom, even if you forgot, how could you have imagined, even for the tiniest moment, that I didn't invite him to our wedding?"

"Well, he wasn't in any of the wedding pictures."

"But why did you leap to such a nasty conclusion?"

I stared out the window at the leaden sky as I waited for the response I knew she wouldn't give.

"And Mom, you wrote that I didn't include him in any of the things we do. I've told you many times I invite him to come to Betty's place or to your place and that we meet him at a restaurant every time we come to Minnesota. Why do you accuse me of something that isn't true?"

"You misunderstood what I wrote."

"No, Mom, I didn't misunderstand. Do you know how many times he's invited us to his house in the past thirteen years? Not even once."

I was done with her accusations. Done with her excuses. Done with trying to get something from her she could not or would not give.

"And, Mom, why do you say you think more of Marvin than you think of me?"

"I don't remember saying that."

"You don't remember?" I unfolded her letter to Betty. "I'm going to read your exact words. Here is what you wrote: 'I think more of Marvin than I think of Marilyn—because she thinks so much of herself.' Now Mom, tell me, how can I possibly misunderstand those words?"

Why was I crying? Hadn't I emptied myself of tears?

A long silence. Then her muted response.

"I don't know why I said such a terrible thing."

"Yes, Mom," I said, my voice sinking into my fatigue. "I do not know why you said such a terrible thing."

CHAPTER 35

The days inched by, stretching into endless nights, as I considered all that had happened in my struggle with Mom. When Paul and I talked about my breaking away from her rules and restrictions, he had said, "You broke out of the prison she tried to keep you in." But I locked myself behind bars of my own making in my struggle to gain her acceptance and love. My resistance to the truth had been formidable. "Too deep," Paul had said. "Too painful."

My fight with Mom and its toll on my relationships and my capacity to be happy had come to an end. I had broken free of my bondage to her.

I did not think she would mention our conversation in her next letter, nor did I expect an apology:

> I am sorry I wrote about you and Marvin—I beg you
> for forgiveness and I shall not do it again. There are
> lots of things an old lady does without thinking.

She had acted "without thinking." Much of what I had learned came from outside the realm of rational thought—memories mined from times long forgotten, emotions pushed aside, dreams generated by my unconscious mind. Mom reacted to what she felt without taking time to think. I allowed my thoughts to overrule what I felt. Her way was too hot. My way was too cold.

Her apology was narrow in scope. A few sentences she had inadvertently written about Marvin and me. It was enough. I no longer needed what she was unable to give.

I had hoped to move on to a new stage in my relationship with Mom, no longer poisoned by our conflicts in the past. But not long after her apology, she began peppering her letters with words of despair:

> Why am I still here? I feel it would be just as good for me to pass away as mother did. I'm older now than she was when she died.

Betty and I drove her to the Mayo Clinic for a complete workup, where the doctors confirmed what we already knew—she had fallen into a major depression. After several months of medication, her depression lifted. But the early signs of memory loss did not go away.

Mom had cared for her mother with generous compassion during the seven years she lived with us. She had followed a strict low-fat diet and adhered to a rigorous exercise program for more than twenty years, hoping to avoid the dementia that ravaged her mother's mind. When she learned of her diagnosis, I wanted to hold her in my arms.

She had cared for me with concern and compassion when I was sick as a child. Now it was my turn to assist in the care she would require.

After an appointment with her doctor, she again picked up her pen:

> July 17, 2000
>
> Dear Marilyn,
>
> I have been interested in knowing and serving the Lord as far back as I remember. I'm not about to quit now. However, the Alzheimer's might take over and leave me not knowing what I'm doing. I want important things said before I get to that stage.
>
> I want all my four children to believe in God. I want them all to love Him and His son Jesus. I want you all to find a church with a great spiritual interest—sing in the choir and take an interest in the Bible.

I started you out in Sunday School when you were about four. One Saturday you had been in bed all day with a fever. You told me I should call your Sunday School teacher and tell her you couldn't be there on Sunday. At that time I thought, "Here's a girl who knows where important studies are." I didn't think you would ever ever ever leave a Sunday without going to a church service. I want you to come back. Locate a church with the right kind of spiritual help, choir, Sunday School, etc. If I can think of you as being a Christian mother, Christian grandmother, you can think of me as the happiest lady you can find—Alzheimer's or no Alzheimer's. This part of my life is what is important to me.

You're a good and fast reader. Get your Bible out and read. I love the book of Luke. I have loved my Lord since as far back as I remember. If you tell me you are attending church, you'll have the happiest mother!!! It will mean so much to me.

Don't feel sorry for me for my health problem. I got some PAXIL pills—take one a day. I love all my family. You were a very good daughter. You took care of the garden when Betty and I had mumps. And you also took care of Mark, which I have told him so many times. He is a very good help to me.

I love you, Marilyn. I always have. I will love you all the more if you take my words seriously. God loves us all—that is wonderful.

Love you, love you, and love you,
MOM Ruby

P.S. Go to a pastor and ask for help. They are trained for this.

She had been able to "take by faith" all she was taught by her parents and her pastors. Her faith comforted her. It gave her strength and filled her with hope. It connected her to her parents, her sisters and brothers, their church community. But she held her convictions so rigidly, she was unable to grant integrity to anyone whose beliefs differed from hers.

Still, I felt in her letter a deep concern for my wellbeing. Perhaps even, beneath her admonitions and instructions, genuine love.

CHAPTER 36

Each time George turned our rental car into the driveway, it was as if we had returned to my childhood. The steel skeleton of the old windmill still towered over the barn, now a faded red, where Mark's sows gave birth to their piglets. The corrugated-steel flag Dad bolted to the top of the windmill to replace the rotating blades continued to turn with the wind, but the stars and stripes I painted on the flag had long since disappeared. A jagged hole had appeared in the roof of the old granary, its wooden shingles drooping like unkempt hair. But the henhouse had taken on a new life. It served as a nursery for Mark's pigs, where he moved them after they were weaned. One of the doors had fallen from the wooden corncrib, where Marvin and I once gathered cobs of corn, pushing them between the boards to the snouts of Dad's squealing white Yorkshire pigs. Mark's Berkshire pigs, with black bodies and white patches on their faces and legs, scrambled in and out of the growing and finishing house he had built on the same spot where Dad's old pig house stood before it caught on fire and burned to the ground.

"What will you do when you retire?" I asked Mark as we sat around their kitchen table. "Are you planning on selling the farm?"

Their son, Davis, had moved to Minneapolis, where he loaded UPS trucks. He had no interest in farming. Their daughter, Angelina, was working towards a PsyD at the Wright Institute in Berkeley, California, with no intention of returning to Minnesota.

Whoever bought the farm would knock down the windmill and the silo, rip down the barn and the machine sheds, tear down the buildings that housed the pigs, and level the granaries, maybe even the house.

"Well, it'll be a long time before that happens," Mark said, his speech still colored with a Swedish brogue. "I'll grow corn and soybeans when I'm done with pigs. I'm a lot younger than you are, you know."

He chuckled. I grimaced.

Each time George and I flew to Minnesota, we visited the farm. But during the holiday week of 2001, we spent our time at the Comfort Inn in Willmar where the family had gathered for a five-day "Grandma Ruby Christmas" celebration.

To reach the opposite side of the lobby, I circled around nieces from the West Coast chatting with their East Coast cousins and stepped over the legs of giggling girls in pink and purple leggings lying on the floor amidst the scent of new crayons. I passed tables where the women were arranging food—platters of sliced ham, bowls of three-bean salad, pieces of chicken from a local deli, red and green Rice Krispies bars, gallon jugs of milk—while crinkling bags and popping lids off plastic containers. After maneuvering between the tables of men arguing about the Super Bowl playoffs, whether the New York Knicks or the Chicago Bulls would win the NBA game, I came face-to-face with Betty, who was staring at the hallway where Marvin had stomped off and disappeared into Sharon's and his room.

"Why was Marvin yelling at you?" I asked. "What is he so upset about?"

"He's mad at you." She pointed a scarlet fingernail at my face.

"What did I do? I've barely had a chance to say hello to him."

"You haven't done anything. He's mad at you for calling the cops fifteen years ago," she said, the ceramic cats in her earrings shuddering above the embroidered cats on her sweater. "I'm really worried—he says you ruined his life!"

Betty had never seen him during one of his manic episodes, even though they had been a recurring pattern for the past fifteen years. None of the others who had gathered for the Grandma Ruby Christmas had noticed his outburst. Few of them knew the symptoms of mania. Fewer yet understood bipolar disorder.

"We're not going!" Marvin had told Sharon when he learned of the plans for the reunion. Everyone else had jumped at the idea when Naomi suggested it.

Even the 9/11 terrorist attack three months earlier—George and I staring open-mouthed at the television screen in our Willmar motel room as the second plane tunneled into the World Trade Center—had not deterred us. We allowed extra time to get through the security lines that snaked through our departure airports—Boston, Los Angeles, San Francisco, Philadelphia, Hartford—with gun-toting guards marching through the holiday crowds.

After Marvin learned that Kristi, a software engineer for IBM in Rochester, Minnesota, was planning to drive to the reunion, he had changed his mind.

When Marvin returned to the reception area, I walked over and stood at his side as he assessed the crowd from the periphery of the room.

"So, Marv, do you think Mom is enjoying the Grandma Ruby Christmas?"

"I want to leave because I want to watch football and no one in this group gives a shit about football!" he said, spitting out the words in one angry blast.

He spun around, turning his back on me, and after striding down the hallway, slammed the door to their room. A few minutes later, Sharon emerged. "We're leaving!" she announced as she marched up to the reception desk, their suitcase thumping behind her. "We should have gone home right after church!" She jammed their receipt into her handbag and trudged over to Mom, relaxing in an overstuffed chair. After muttering a fast goodbye, she bumped their suitcase out the door, Marvin behind her.

Betty balanced a plate of food on Mom's lap and walked over to me.

"Mom wanted to know why Marvin and Sharon left so quickly," she said.

"What did you tell her?"

"I told her the truth. She should remember Marvin is sick. He is sick again. He is very angry. And he needs to go home."

"What did she say to that?"

"Nothing. She just looked confused."

A year earlier, Mom had ranted to anyone who would listen—"Marilyn is trying to put me in a home!" But she forgot to take her blood pressure pills, forgot to put the drops in her eyes for glaucoma, forgot she had cancelled meals-on-wheels and then fussed when they no longer delivered her dinners. She hallucinated during a bout of the flu, frightening her neighbors by going into a panic over imagined guests from Sweden who hadn't arrived for an imagined visit.

After succumbing to our pleas, she had discovered that she loved living in Sunrise Village, an assisted living facility.

Mom smiled easily as she relaxed amidst the tables and chairs in the reception area at the Comfort Inn. She laughed at her eighteen-month-old great-grandson, Winston, who couldn't resist running water from the spigot on the water dispenser, and pointed a pink-enameled fingernail at each of the photographs of her grandchildren and great-grandchildren—"Oh, look, doesn't he have a cute smile!"—in the albums and scrapbooks we had made for her.

Marvin and Sharon's hasty departure did not upset her. It upset me.

"I so wanted this to be a fun time for Kristi," I said to George, "for us to finally have a chance to get to know her. Why did Marvin have to wreck everything?"

"I had a chance to talk to Kristi. She didn't seem at all concerned."

"What did she say?"

"That Marvin and Sharon would go home, he'd go back on his medications, and on Monday morning, he'd be back at work."

"Is she heading back to Rochester?"

"No. She plans on staying all five days."

Kristi stayed all five days of the Grandma Ruby Christmas reunion, but Marvin did not return to work the following Monday. A week after their abrupt departure, mania-driven hallucinations took over his mind. He lashed out at Sharon, insisting she was the one who was sick, as he tried to prevent her from dialing 911. He refused to sign a release to give her access to his medical information, rejected her attempts to participate in his care. After a week in the psychiatric ward, while still in a state of mania, he checked himself out of the hospital.

Worried about her own safety and worn down by the increasing frequency and intensity of his cycle of depressive and manic episodes, Sharon moved out of their home. They had been married thirty years when she filed for a divorce.

By chance, I had called Mom the evening Marvin tried to prevent Sharon from dialing 911. He had driven to Willmar that day to visit her.

"We went to a bunch of stores," she said. "We didn't stay long at any of them. I don't know what he was looking for."

"Did you stop for lunch?" I asked, after she described a string of visits to relatives and a stop at the Rice Memorial Hospital to visit our uncle Kermit Holmgren.

"No, I don't remember eating."

When I telephoned her a week later, she said Kermit had been released from the hospital and was back in his room at Sunrise Village.

"He made a point of telling me how much he appreciated what Marvin had said as we walked out of his room in the hospital," she said.

"What did Marvin say?" I asked.

"He said, 'Pray for me, Kermit—and I'll pray for you.'" She had thought for a moment before saying, "I never knew Marvin was going to turn out so good."

CHAPTER 37

*M*arvin refused to go to a doctor—except to his psychiatrist when he had to renew his prescriptions. After their divorce, Sharon arranged for his medical care to be transferred to the Minneapolis VA Medical Center, where they required him to have a physical. Their tests revealed prostate cancer.

He told their longtime friends, Sina and Bill Kude, about the diagnosis. He did not inform anyone in our family.

Six months after the diagnosis, during Mom's ninetieth birthday party, he told our family about the cancer. He did not tell us that it was aggressive and advanced. "I'm not a candidate for surgery," was the only information he would reveal when I asked about his treatment plan. Several months after the party, he underwent a regimen of radiation therapy.

Two years after the radiation treatments, during one of our telephone conversations, he mentioned a gush of blood in his urine. I pressed him to call his doctor. He waited until his next regularly scheduled appointment, after which he sent me a postcard. He had mailed it on May 18, 2006:

The doctor said it may have been from a damaged bladder or my prostate gland. My bladder could have been zapped when I had radiation therapy.

But I no longer trusted what he said. The information frequently differed from what he had told me previously. "Marvin, I'm confused. You said before that your PSA was seventy-four. Now you're saying it was seventeen?" I questioned his ability to communicate with his doctors, his capacity to make informed judgments about his medical care, whether the staff at the VA Medical Center had obtained his records from the St. Paul-Ramsey Medical Center and was aware of his psychiatric history. Despite the debilitating impact of mental illness, he had the right to make his own medical decisions. I knew if I tried to intervene in his medical care, he would explode with anger.

I wanted to help my brother, but I did not know how.

During the next two years, he had several more surges of blood, which he claimed to have reported to his doctors. A routine urinalysis revealed red blood cells in his urine. The follow-up procedures indicated a carcinoma in his kidney and urethra. His doctors scheduled surgery to remove the cancerous kidney.

I had always called him, but he began calling me. He talked non-stop as he worried about losing a kidney. I worried about his increasing mania. If he ended up in a psychiatric ward, the surgery would be postponed, he would go through another stress-filled period while waiting for the rescheduled surgery, his stress would trigger another manic episode, and the surgery would again be postponed. Meanwhile, the cancer would advance.

His calls came more frequently. His speech grew more frenzied.

I scanned the internet to find the doctor whose name I had tricked Marvin into mentioning. "I'm the twin of one of your patients," I said, surprised that he answered his own phone. I described Marvin's anxiety over the impending surgery, his increasing mania, a history of psychiatric hospitalizations.

The doctor promised to have someone on Marvin's medical team check his mental status. He assured me he understood the need to keep my intervention confidential.

Marvin put it together immediately. "I'm never going to tell her anything ever again!" he raged in a telephone call to Betty. He recorded a message on his answering machine telling me to stop calling him as he was "never ever again" going to take a call from me.

I had violated his trust in me. Instead of helping him, I had ignited his rage.

I wrote a letter and apologized. He rejected my apology.

His kidney surgery occurred, as had been scheduled. Four weeks later, he returned to the VA Medical Center for follow-up chemotherapy. Instead of receiving the first treatment, his doctors diagnosed a major depression. They admitted him to 1K, the inpatient mental health center.

Marvin called it "the lockdown ward."

Two weeks after he was admitted to the VA Medical Center, a ten-minute drive from the Minneapolis-St. Paul airport, George and I trekked down a labyrinth of halls surrounding a large atrium, lined with trees and benches, until we found the inpatient mental health center, where we pushed a buzzer to have the door unlocked. A nurse asked us to leave our coats, packages, and my shoulder bag at their station. We walked past a succession of empty hospital rooms until we found a large common room where Marvin and one other man, both dressed in purple pajamas and purple robes, were sitting in front of a television screen.

"Marvin, we've come to visit you," I said.

He looked stunned when he heard my voice. With one arm unbending at his side, he shuffled across the room to greet us. After fourteen days in 1K, he would have been happy to see any familiar face.

A nurse led us to a sitting room. Marvin propped his elbows on top of the small round table as George and I sat across from him.

I studied his face while we gently prodded him with questions.

"So you had a chance to try meals-on-wheels. How did you like their food?"

"It was okay."

"Do you plan on going back to work at Cub, once you get out of the hospital?"

"Maybe. If I feel strong enough."

His eyes, as blue as when we ran through the pigweed, had lost their luster. His face looked listless, his cheeks as colorless as his brows and lashes. His tics, still present, were subdued.

"Will you vote for Hillary—if she beats Obama in the primary?" I asked, searching for a topic that might ignite his interest. "Some people really hate her."

"I might vote for her. But I don't talk politics."

His fingers trembled as he braced them against his chin. His fingernails were long, in need of a trim.

"What do you hear from Kristi? I hear she spent lots of time helping you after your surgery."

"She's okay."

"How does she like her job at IBM? It should be a good place to work."

"She seems to think it's okay."

I felt his weariness. It was as if we were trying to drag him out of some deep, dark place.

"I hear she has a pet rabbit. Does it get along with Bluey? When we were growing up, our cats snacked on any rabbits they could run down," I said, hoping to spark a light in his eyes. "Do you remember that time Mom let us keep two baby rabbits as pets?"

Dad had tucked the little cottontails into the toolbox of his tractor and built a chicken wire pen for them. Marvin carried one end of the pen and I the other as we moved them to a fresh patch of grass each day. We lay on our bellies and fed them clover while we stroked their soft backs.

But one fall day, after we returned from the one-room school, I ran to the pen and found that it was empty. "I don't know how they could have gotten out!" I had said to Mom, trying to understand how both of our tame rabbits could have escaped from such a sturdy pen.

"I never suspected, never gave it a thought, that Mom might have let them go," I said, still surprised at her deception. "I didn't find out until long after—it was decades later. She said they hung around our yard for weeks."

Marvin chuckled. He dropped his fingers from his cheek.

"Kristi lets her rabbit run around her house. It gets along fine with Bluey."

He looked directly at me, the first time he had made eye contact since we sat down.

"Kristi said I was depressed—but I didn't know I was depressed."

She had struggled to get him to leave the recliner in his living room while caring for him during his recovery from kidney surgery but was unable to talk him into changing into regular clothes or to spur him to walk from room to room to build up his strength.

Before he went to the VA Medical Center for his first chemotherapy treatment, she had called his home nurse and asked her to alert his doctors to his depressed mood.

"Marvin, you have ample reason to be depressed," I said, "given you're still recovering from surgery and with a bunch of chemotherapy ahead of you."

"Yes, but lots of people wouldn't understand that."

He had suffered through repeated hospitalizations for psychotic episodes, radiation treatments for prostate cancer, and multiple invasive procedures, as well as kidney surgery. And yet, he was worried about the stigma of depression.

I remembered how his weary eyes had glistened as we built dams in front of our henhouse, scooping up pebbles and mounding up mud as the rain spilled down our faces; how we shrieked with glee as the water burst through our barrier; how his fingers, now pale and shaky, were coated with mud as he gripped the handle of Mom's kitchen strainer, pulling it through the stream in Bengtson's pasture and dumping the minnows into our bucket of water; the joy in his laughter as we had dumped the minnows into the cows' watering tank, thinking they would eat the clumps of moss that floated on the water and grow big enough for us to catch with Chester's fishing poles.

None of us had thought of the possibility of depression when he struggled to wake up in time to catch the bus to the town school, or as he lay across his bed when Dad wanted him to help with the work. I had little tolerance for his lethargy. Dad had none.

How different might our relationships have been if his depression had been diagnosed while we were in high school?

The nurse, having looked in at us several times while we chatted, peered into the room as we stood up to leave. Marvin skidded his slippered feet along the floor as we returned to the common room, arm unbending in his purple robe. His ankles looked swollen.

"I'm sorry we can't stay longer," I said. "If you're still here on our way back from visiting Mom, we'll stop in to see you again."

He felt tense as I hugged him. We had squeezed together in a crowded uterus, intertwined our legs in a claw-foot tub, rubbed shoulders as we examined a toad, but my touch now made him uneasy.

My brother's loneliness, his shrunken world, pressed down on me as the door to 1K locked behind us.

CHAPTER 38

The dazzling rays of the August sun shimmered through the open windows of the Salem Evangelical Covenant Church as the electric organ spilled a tremulous sweetness across the pews. A breeze, wafting an aroma of ripened grain, rippled in from the surrounding fields as I stretched my vocal cords, thick from neglect, to sing the words my grandparents and great-grandparents had sung in Swedish:

> Day by day and with each passing moment,
> Strength I find to meet my trials here....

Relatives and friends who had gathered to celebrate my mother's long life sang from the hymnals. I sang from my memory. When we turned to one of her favorite hymns, "The Old Rugged Cross," I remembered sitting beside her on the bench of our old upright piano, her fingers gliding across the keys as she filled our home with the familiar gospel melodies. When Mark stepped into the pulpit to deliver our family tribute, I closed my eyes. He sounded just like Dad.

Pastor McCain, knowing Mom's love of writing and her passion for family, had entitled his meditation, "I Love to Tell the Story," another of her favorite hymns. He had let us plan the service as if it was 1951 and she was sitting in a pew six rows behind us, her black feathered hat pinned to her pumpkin-colored hair.

He had visited her in the Rice Care Center nursing home several times a week for the past two and a half years, laughing as they shared stories, breaking up her long days with his generous spirit. And Pastor Melvie had visited her at the nursing home during the four years before that, and at Sunrise Village for the year prior to that, driving her to LuLu Beans and chatting with her over a cup of gourmet coffee.

Her last roommate at the Rice Care Center had greeted George and me with a friendly "hello" each time we walked into the room. I would wake Mom, dozing in her easy chair, sometimes napping on her bed, by lightly stroking her arm.

"Marilyn," she would say, opening her eyes as I leaned down to kiss her cheek. "George," as she clasped his hand in hers.

I fluffed the curls—as white as the clouds above her when she weeded the beets and beans—that softened her pale cheeks. The half-frame glasses, which I helped her select, suited her face.

George strolled on one side of her, I on the other, as she edged her walker down the hallway on our way to the sitting room. I felt protective of her, watching out for her as we stepped aside for the wheelchairs, the oxygen tanks, the medicine cart. She thanked the caregiver who brought her fresh water and praised the one who helped her with her bath, eliciting tenderness from those who cared for her. I felt warmed by her gentle and gracious spirit, the mother I had wanted, the mother she had become.

"I don't remember so many bedrooms in my mother's house," she said, glancing into each of the rooms as we made our way down the hallway.

In her mother's house, she had lived with her parents, her four sisters and four brothers, and her mother's sister Lottie. All of them, in her mind, were still alive. "My parents usually sit in the back," she said, turning her head to search the pews for Hjalmar and Maria when we drove her to Sunday morning services; "Mom and Dad haven't visited me recently. They must be in Sweden. I think they're on vacation," as we chatted on our drives to the farm; "Our marriage must have gone bad; Winston never comes to see me," a puzzled look on her face as she sipped tiny sips of coffee in the sitting room.

"Mom, you don't remember," I would say. "Dad died of cancer. You were so good to him. There wasn't anything more you could have done. He loved you very much."

"Oh. I guess I've forgotten that."

But we stopped reminding her of Dad's death, of the deaths of the many people she had loved, as it plunged her into renewed grief. She drew comfort from thinking her sister Olga was busy at her job in Minneapolis, her parents were enjoying a vacation in Sweden—a trip they never took.

Mom rode in the front and I in the back when George drove along the country roads. We chatted about the height of the corn, if there had been enough rain, who had lived on the farms while she was growing up. When we stepped out of the car at our farm, she leaned down to pet Noodle, Mark and Sue's little dachshund. Mark brought Noodle and a small bag of Cheerios with him on his visits to the Rice Care Center. Mom extracted each Cheerio from the bag and circled it around the dog's nose before dropping it into its mouth, a game Noodle also enjoyed.

When our visits with Mark and Sue ended, George would turn out the driveway onto the gravel road heading east. "Where are we going?" Mom would ask, wondering why we hadn't turned into the driveway to the retirement house, where she thought she still lived and which Mark now rented out.

On one sun-washed afternoon, as Mom and I rested on a bench in the courtyard behind the Rice Care Center, she turned to me with a quizzical look.

"You remind me so much of my daughter Marilyn," she said.

"But Mom," I gently protested, "I *am* Marilyn."

"Oh, you're Marilyn too—there are two Marilyns."

I stayed abreast of the latest Alzheimer's medications, reviewing the information with Mark, who discussed them with Mom's doctor when he drove her to her appointments. I squeezed new photographs of her great-grandchildren onto her bulletin boards that overflowed with family pictures. Each week I wrote a letter, numbering the pages on the upper right-hand corner. But during our last visit, I found my letters, unopened, on her night table. She no longer had the strength to slip her index finger under the flap to break the seal.

I had wanted to sit at the kitchen table as she sipped coffee and I sipped tea and discuss the news about our relatives, her friends, my classmates, our neighbors on the farm. I wanted to laugh with her, to bathe myself in the love I had uncovered, to travel together down an easier road.

But our time had run out as dementia chipped away her memory, chipped away her mind, chipped away her capacity to respond. I felt a deep loss as she slipped away.

In August of 2008, two months after her ninety-fourth birthday, Mark called to alert us to her weakening condition. Our daughter Stephanie flew in from her home in London and cradled her grandmother's hand as she talked of the times that she had sneaked sugar cubes from her sugar bowl, how much she had loved reading our old stack of comic books while sitting on the porch of the retirement house. George spoke of our many visits to the farm, his deep voice filled with love and caring as he thanked her for the endless pots of coffee she had brewed. I thanked her for the treasure hunts she planned, the picnics she prepared to take to the lake on Sunday afternoons, the many parties she helped me arrange for our cousins and friends, as I stroked the soft flesh on her arm.

When she closed her eyes and slipped into silence, I caressed the back of her hand. I wept for all we had said, and for all we had never been able to say.

A stillness blanketed the room as we had leaned over her bed, listening to her breathing as it slowed. Listening to her breathing as it stopped.

Pastor McCain closed his Bible. He asked us to turn to the closing hymn, page 775, in the hymnals. I sang the words as a tribute to Mom's enduring faith:

> When we all get to Heaven,
> What a day of rejoicing that will be!

When we all see Jesus,
We'll sing and shout the victory.

Our cousins greeted Marvin at the reception as he surveyed the tables from the side of the fellowship hall in the basement of the church. I wanted to alert them to his favorite topics—Cub Foods, his vehicle, the Vikings, the thistles in his lawn. When he felt at ease, his sense of humor sometimes bubbled through, and he laughed the laugh that had made me laugh too.

I asked if he was planning to spend the afternoon with the family.

"Oh no. I can't stay. I've got too much work to do. I have to cut my grass. I have chores in my house. I have to get to bed early, because I have to go to work at Cub tomorrow."

He did not mention the stress of spending time with our extended family, of mingling with a crowd. Nor did he mention the chemotherapy treatments and the blood transfusions and the diagnostic tests scheduled for the end of the week.

His body felt taut, unyielding, as I hugged him, as if taken aback by the physicality of my embrace. I sensed his desire to escape from the funeral of a mother who had always championed him, from a loss he wanted to push aside.

After our time with the family had ended, George and I and our children returned to the farm. I still expected the house to be white, even though Mark and Sue had painted it a gold-tinged beige with ruby-colored trim thirty-five years earlier. The flowerbeds where I knelt beside Mom when she planted her petunias and marigolds were now lush with Sue's hydrangeas and phlox. The long porch across the front of the house, where Marvin and I rounded the corners on two wheels of our tricycles, had been refurbished into a large deck. They no longer used the entryway where Dad pulled off his four-buckle overshoes. Not long after Mark and Sue moved in, they had relocated the kitchen to where the living room had been.

"She won't be able to look out the kitchen window and see what's going on in the barn!" Mom had said, shaking her head.

The sun hovered above the horizon, streaming long shadows behind the tombstones, when we drove back to the cemetery. A breeze rustled the leaves of the boxelder trees as we strolled past the graves of Mom's parents, her brothers and sisters, nieces and nephews who had died too young.

After watering the marigolds she planted in front of her father's headstone, Mom had liked to wander through the cemetery. "Here is Lottie's grave," she would say. "Here is Uncle Adolph's." Marvin and I had cupped our hands to capture grasshoppers and frogs.

Now the grasshoppers rasped and the crickets chirped as we walked further back in the cemetery to the tombstones eroded by the wind and rain. A vertical headstone marked the grave of Mom's grandfather Karl Jonsson Johnson. A few weeks earlier, the first of the seventh generation of Johnsons had been born.

We circled back to the headstone hewn from Minnesota granite with "PETERSON" engraved between two sprays of wheat. The crows called from a nearby wood as we bowed our heads before the newly mounded prairie soil.

Our son, Nik, thanked Mom for overlooking the messes he had made while crawling through the long, dark closet that connected the upstairs bedrooms in the retirement house, for allowing him to eat her oatmeal raisin cookies straight from the freezer. Our daughter Naomi thanked her for the traits she had passed on to her great-grandchildren—a love of writing to Clara, an enthusiastic spirit to Winston, the bright smile that lit up little Henry's face.

I told her how much I would miss her.

CHAPTER 39

I felt mortified to be dialing Paul's number. In my holiday card, I had included a letter telling him about my mother's death and how my love had felt bigger than our troubled relationship, bigger than the things we needed to forgive. "After her final breath, my spirit felt calm and cleansed," I wrote.

I wanted it to be so. But I had begun to erupt in outbursts at the people I loved—most of all, at my children.

Feeling anything but calm and cleansed, I clamped my hands in a tight knot as I watched Paul from across the low square table. His dark eyes had retained their intensity, but his black hair had softened with an inroad of white during the seventeen years since my therapy had ended.

Instead of easing into a conversation, I spouted out a description of the way I had been flying into torrents of angry words, denigrating things that were important to our children, that it had happened again during their holiday visit. "I don't know what's wrong with me. It's like I have this huge reservoir of rage. It just builds up, and no matter what I do, I can't seem to stop myself!" I said, reaching for the box of tissues.

"It's been a very difficult time for you. Your mother's death is still fresh in your memory. Your brother's condition is weighing heavily on your mind. Add to this the stress of having the entire family in your house for a week? It's remarkable that's *all* that happened!"

I unclenched my hands.

"But I don't understand why I'm having these outbursts. I'm going to wreck my relationships with my children. I've got to find a way to stop myself—if I don't, that's what's going to happen!"

"Your mother died only a few months ago," he said, as I reached for another tissue. "There's a belief that you channel a person you've been close to for four seasons after they die, while their spirit looks for a place to rest."

The tissue melded into a lump in my hand. I had no time for spirits floating through the air, scouting about for a place to live. The channeling thing was too New Age-y for me. Paul often surprised me with his openness to different ways of perceiving the world. I responded to new ways of thinking with a cynical mind, insisting on a double-blind study with unbiased data to substantiate a process known as channeling. And yet, he had introduced me to the world of dreams, with no confirmed explanation of how a dream transports unconscious emotions and repressed memories to the conscious mind.

"Or you may be channeling your mother's characteristics," he said. "Especially her bad ones."

An icy shudder shot across my chest as I realized I had been behaving like my mother. I had scorned my son's use of a homeopathic remedy, demonstrating a high level of intolerance over the type of ointment he reached for in order to sooth his children's bruises. I attacked my children when their beliefs differed from mine, revealing an inability to grant credence to other ways of viewing the world. I slid down in my chair.

"Your twin lost your mother, his protector. You still feel guilty about your brother—you may have taken over her role as his protector."

I gripped the lump of tissues in my hand as I thought about the many calls I had made to monitor Marvin after Mom's death.

"Or you may be channeling your brother and his rages, even more than your mother's."

"I don't understand," I said. "Why would his rages have anything to do with me attacking my children?"

He braced his chin on his fingertips as he considered his response.

I glanced at the papers stacked on his desk, the books lined up on his shelves, his collection of pebbles on the table, as I wondered what concepts he might be considering, what insights might flash through his mind.

He dropped his hands to his lap.

"In some unconscious cosmic sense, you may be trying to destroy everything around you, the relationships you value the most, in order to equalize things with your twin."

A jolt of heat shot up my spine. "Destroy what I love? My relationships with my children?" My heart felt as if it was trying to escape from my chest. "Why would anyone do something so ridiculous? Something so absurd?"

Paul's eyes filled with warmth, and tenderness.

"*Marilyn,*" he said. "*Your twin is part of you.*"

After swiveling the faucets on our claw-foot tub, I closed my eyes and slid into the warmth of the lemon-scented water. Could Paul be right? I had included my twin as part of my own being?

I knew twins were at risk of having a "diffuse boundary." When they reach the developmental stage at which they are to define themselves as separate individuals, they have a tendency to include their twin as part of their own identity. As a result, they may end up with an unclear sense of where their "self" ends and their twin's "self" begins. But I had never imagined these issues applied to me. When Mom told me I swallowed the cough syrup to make Marvin well, I thought of it as nothing more than a cute story. I never wondered why I cried when he was scolded. Nor did I think it unusual that when someone teased him, it was as if they were teasing me.

Paul once said, "When you and your twin are in the same room, you are not in your own self; you are with him." At the time, I did not know what he meant. But when I saw Marvin walk into the funeral home after Mom's death, I felt as if I, too, had just walked into the room that held our mother's coffin. His anxiety became my anxiety as he stood in front of the larkspurs, examining them as a ruse while bracing himself to converse with our relatives.

When I walked out of 1K, a part of me had remained behind the locked door. Part of me had drowned when the twin I loved slipped under the water.

As I slid further down into the fragrant embrace of my bath, I thought about diffuse boundaries. Our thinking mind crosses a line that separates our conscious and unconscious thoughts when we fall asleep, giving our dreaming mind control during the night. But I had seen that line breached as my brother's unconscious mind refused to relinquish its authority in the morning, allowing his nightmares to hold their control over him during the day.

I had believed a definitive boundary existed between what is true and what is false. No matter how complex an issue, I considered a stance to be right or wrong. That the world is made up of absolute good and absolute evil. People are either saved or doomed.

But as Paul wrote on my insurance form, my black-and-white mindset left me "unprepared for the flexibility required of adult family life," my way of thinking "insufficient for adapting to a complex world."

I realized that opposite truths could coexist. A father who cradled piglets in his palms could also chase them up a ramp to be slaughtered. The same hands that guided a calf's mouth to a teat could lift an axe while centering a rooster's neck on a stump. He could kill newborn kittens to keep our place from being overrun by cats. I could love my twin at the same time as I hated his beard.

As I sank further into the water, my ears slid beneath the surface. The sound of my heart pulsed against my ears. In my first bath, an amniotic bath, I had heard a second heartbeat intertwined with the sound of mine.

How was I to separate the heart that belonged to my twin from the one that belonged to me?

Paul and I agreed that a third visit was all that would be need-ed—a final session to wrap up any lingering issues.

"I've been thinking," I said, tossing my shoulder bag beside my chair. "If Mom was a good mother 95 percent of the time, why would the other 5 percent be so important?"

A flash of disbelief shot across his eyes. I wondered why he was taken aback by my question.

"It's not the portion of her energy that's important," he said, "but where she aimed her energy."

"I don't understand."

"Your mother took aim at your success. She couldn't stand for you to be successful, to be a leader, to look like you were going to achieve. You defied the role of a woman in Christianity—especially when her son was supposed to be successful. You assumed the role she believed rightly belonged to him."

I had thought my mother resented my achievements because she believed I had become arrogant. But her disparaging words had come from a far deeper place. She wanted me to talk less because my broth-er's thoughts were more important than mine. She denigrated my career because his work was to have greater value. She had to smash me down and make me look small because she believed my successes diminished him.

"Your mother could be vicious," Paul said. "When you tried to break away from her, to be yourself, you brought down her wrath."

The word "vicious" shocked me. Never had I thought of my mother as being cruel. And yet, each time I stepped away from her religious beliefs, she had tried to strike me down.

I had castigated women who strove to please the men who con-trolled them with anger. I belittled them for being weak, for not stand-ing up for themselves. But I had spent six decades trying to please a mother who controlled me with her anger. Rather than standing up for myself, I cowered in fear of her retaliation. I had acted no differ-ently than the women I disparaged.

Paul glanced at the clock. My session had come to an end. "It's psychologically very hip to limit the negative to 5 percent," he said, smiling as I reached for my shoulder bag.

On my drive home, I wondered if he thought my 95 percent question had been unwitting and naive, that I was making light of the despair that had landed me in his office. But I was not about to whitewash the intensity of my struggle, the anguish I had suffered in my search for the sources of my pain.

When I was planning a party to celebrate Mom's ninetieth birthday, Betty had asked, "Why are you being so nice to Mom when she's been so mean to you?"

Her question had caused me to consider my motivation. Perhaps I was acting out an ancient twin-myth theme in a competition for a parent's blessing. Maybe I wanted to give her a party after all the birthday parties she had given for Marvin and me. I may have wanted to give her a party because I knew how much she loved parties.

Or perhaps I had discovered that, beneath my anger, I still loved her.

CHAPTER 40

had not had time to read the pages in Marvin's baby book at the time Kristi pulled the small white box with a blue border from her tote bag. I noted that his book had an identical spray of apple blossoms as had been embossed on the padded satin cover of my book, but the satin on his was blue rather than pink.

As soon as George and I returned to Lenox, I wrapped myself in a comforter and opened the copy we had made of Marvin's book. Mom's slanted script spilled across all sixteen pages. She had squeezed in paragraphs above the headers, wedged sentences into the spaces between the entries, and packed the last four pages with stories— spaces that were empty in my book.

I turned to the page where she documented Marvin's first steps. It was as I expected. She made it sound as if both of us had walked at the exact same time:

> [A]t fourteen months and two weeks he, as well as
> his sister, walked alone quite well and kept improving.

On the page where she recorded his first word, she wrote that he said "Mama" at the exact same age as I had said "Mama." He put together his first sentence when he was two and a half, the exact same age I had put together a few words.

But I no longer trusted her entries. Did I "wait" for my twin to talk in the same way I had "waited" for him to walk?

I scanned through the pages until I came to the one for describing our birthday parties. She listed the guests who attended—Karen and Bruce, Faith and Dale; the foods she served—ice cream, cake, scalloped potatoes, meat sandwiches; the gifts we received—we each got a doll and Marvin loved his dolly. All the spaces for our first seven parties had been embellished with details.

I threw my comforter aside and pulled my pink book from the shelf in our bookcase. In my book, the spaces for information about our parties had been left blank after our second year.

Each time I confronted additional evidence that my mother had favored my brother, I felt my neck flush. But I no longer exploded in a rage. We had been trapped in a crosscurrent of expectations—a father whose heart was set on a firstborn son who looked forward to taking over the family farm, a firstborn son who was unwilling to take on the mantle of his birthright, a mother who tried to make her son into the son they had wanted, a daughter who was unwilling to allow her mother to control her life.

Rather than rage, I felt sorrow. Sorrow for each of us.

I turned to the spaces Mom had filled with stories. His love of naps; the time he tried to carry a cat but was unable to get both ends off the floor; his favorite foods—soup, oatmeal, rice pudding; the way he loved to "hammer and saw" after they gave him a tool set of his own.

But I sat up as I read one of the stories:

> During his first two years of living, Marvin had to pack his suitcase and do much visiting as mother got sick off and on. He and Marilyn stayed with Alice and Paul for two weeks one time and several days another time. They did not get lonesome and seldom cried.
>
> When mother went to the hospital for an operation when they were two years and three months old, they were Grandma Peterson's "kiddies" for three weeks—and they were good then too.

Did she believe the words she had written? That toddlers, not yet able to string two words together, would be able to understand their mother would return each time she vanished? That after being dropped off at the home of her brother and his wife—strangers to them—for two weeks and a second time for several days, they wouldn't feel as if they had been abandoned? And then left with their grandmother for another three weeks with no sign of their mother coming back—how could she have imagined that we "did not get lonesome"?

I had forgotten the stories about her attacks of gallbladder disease, when she was too sick to get out of bed and had to find someone to care for her children. "My brother Paul couldn't believe how good the two of you were," she said, pleased with how good we were when she had traveled to Minneapolis and spent nine days in the Swedish Hospital, pleased with how good we were when she spent another seven days at her Uncle Alfred's home in Minneapolis before she was able to make the trip home, happy with how good we were when she spent another week at home to recover her strength before we were brought back to our house, glad for how well it had all worked out.

After our first grandchild, Clara, was born, Mom had written a letter telling me about Dr. Dowswell's instructions when Marvin and I were born—that she was not to hold her twins because babies would become spoiled if you held them:

> Each baby was changed into clean diapers, put back in the buggy and given a six-ounce bottle of formula. I'm glad the "style" changed. Now babies are to be cuddled.

I thought about an infant who was not to be held by her mother. A toddler who was separated from her mother for weeks at a time. How that toddler might have felt as if she had been forgotten by her mother. Why she might have felt an anguish so deep and so painful it had to be buried in her unconscious where no one, not even a therapist, could excavate it.

I realized what my dreaming mind had been dredging up from my earliest unconscious memories:

I was the forgotten daughter who inhabited my dreams.

How many stories did I have to uncover? How many memories did I have to surface? How many dreams did I have to dream before I was prepared to face the reality of all that had been revealed?

Two infants longing for the touch of a mother. Two children bonded together in the isolation of a farm. Parents molded by a history of hardships, steered by a rigid set of beliefs. A mental illness that afflicted one twin but affected us all. A mother who tried to fix things for her son by knocking her daughter down.

Marvin and I had each other. But I needed my mother.

CHAPTER 41

My cell phone flashed 12:40 a.m., January 30, 2009, as I paced around the baggage-claim area in the deserted Minneapolis-St. Paul airport while waiting for the carousel to cough up George's and my bags. The guard at the security entrance at the Minneapolis VA Medical Center stifled a yawn as he glanced at our driver's licenses and waved us to a nearby elevator. A trail of signs led us down a maze of hallways to 3L, a brightly lit medical ward, where I stroked my brother's arm to wake him, the same way I had stroked my mother's arm six months earlier.

"Kristi told me you were coming," he said, squinting in the bright overhead lights.

His voice sounded scratchy. His cheeks, clean-shaven, exposed the narrow face I had watched from across the old kitchen table while the aroma of Mom's homemade waffles infused the kitchen.

"What happened to your beard?" I asked.

"I asked them to trim it—they must have misunderstood."

I was sorry to have asked. He loved the thick bristle that masked half his face, mutating over the past several years from the color of rust to the color of milk.

"Is it all right if I hold your hand?" I ventured.

"It's all right, I suppose," he said, easing his hand out from under the sheet.

I remembered how he had eased his hands into the holes along the banks of the creek when we searched for crayfish, Bengtson's long-horned cows following us with their dark eyes as they ripped up tufts of grass. The stream spilled around our ankles as we hopscotched from one stone to the next, and when the sun dipped toward the west, we had dashed back and forth through the big cement culvert on our way home.

"Why didn't you tell anyone you were in the hospital?" I asked, the skin of his palm soft against mine. "We could have come sooner."

"I didn't want to bother you."

For nearly a week he had eluded us, leaving no messages, not answering his phone. But his manager at Cub Foods knew where he had gone. Marvin had called him to report that he wouldn't be at work the remainder of that week, and perhaps not the following week either.

The night nurses streamed in and out, adjusting his pillows, bringing a fresh glass of ice water, testing whether a change in medication might calm his raspy cough.

"It's 3:30 in the morning," I said, glancing at my watch. "We've got to get some sleep. We're going to Betty's. We'll be back in a few hours." I slipped my hand out from his.

When we returned, he slid his hand out from under the sheet.

"I've been waiting for you," he said.

Kristi swept her long hair, as straight and blonde as her father's and mine, away from her face as Betty sat down beside Sharon and her. Unknown to Marvin, Sharon had monitored his medical tests through their friends, Bill and Sina, who had continued to invite him for holiday dinners and to cheer the Vikings in front of their television set. He had shared with them the medical information he kept from us.

Spots in his bladder. Spots in his spine. Spots in his lungs.

The nurses lugged in more chairs as Mark and Sue walked into the room. Sue passed out packages of lefse, soft, thin rounds like Grandma Peterson had flipped on top of her black cast-iron, coal-burning stove. Their son, Davis, stopped by and held Marvin's hand while they chatted about the Pittsburg Steelers and the Arizona Cardinals and which team would win the Super Bowl—Marvin's favorite sports event. Our double cousin Jerry arrived, and soon after, his sister, Margaret, and her husband, Bruce. We laughed about the bicycle trail we had spent weeks building in the woods behind our machine shed, old tires as potholes, a wooden plank as a narrow bridge, a discarded metal headboard for a section of bumpy washboard. When Bill and Sina and their two daughters walked through the doorway, Bill turned aside to wipe his eyes.

"There's no one to call," Marvin had told the nurses after he drove himself to the hospital. "No one to notify."

Even though he appeared to be asleep, I knew he was listening to our conversations. "Do you remember when you talked the Gamble Store into taking your old beat-up bike?" I said. "That old worn-out hand-me-down you had. You used it as a trade-in for a new Schwinn. Do you remember that?"

"Yes, but I don't think it was a Schwinn," he said, without opening his eyes. "I'm pretty sure it was a Hiawatha."

I held in front of him the photo album "For My Womb-Mate" that I had made, completing it a few days before George and I boarded the plane to Minneapolis. I had combed through Mom's old albums to find photographs from the time we were born until he joined the army and I graduated from college. In one, we were wearing matching sweaters and bonnets as we peered at the camera from our walkers. In another, we were dressed in matching sailor suits while holding opposite sides of a plate, tilting at a precarious angle, that held a two-layered birthday cake. I had hoped we'd be able to laugh together as we studied the photographs. But I hurried through the pages as he struggled to focus his eyes.

"That was terrific," he said when I closed the book and gave it to Kristi. It was the same phrase Dad had used when something pleased him.

The next morning, Kristi looked apologetic as she reached into her tote and pulled out a book of photographs she had come across on a closet shelf in Marvin's house. I did not know Mom had already filled a photo album for him. One picture was taken when we were nine months old, Dad balancing him on one knee and me on the other. "Oh my god!" I said, as I looked at another photograph I'd never seen. "Look at this—the two of us standing beside Betty on the running board of our 1938 Ford!"

As we sat beside his bed, two days blurred into three. Three into four. His silences occurred more frequently. They lasted longer.

"It's time to say the things you want to say," the chaplain said.

CHAPTER 42

Sharon eased her arm around Kristi's shoulder as Pastor Beebe leaned his tall frame over the sturdy wooden pulpit and spoke of the swings from the highs of mania to the lows of depression that Marvin had endured. He talked about the eight hospitalizations for psychotic breakdowns and the estrangement his mental illness had inflicted on those around him.

I scanned the faces in the pews—Peterson cousins, Johnson cousins, second cousins, double cousins—wondering how many of our relatives knew my brother had suffered from bipolar I disorder. As long as he and Mom were alive, we had not been free to speak of it.

Pastor Beebe's somber face rounded into a smile as he recounted the story of when Marvin had said he was no longer going to sing in the church choir because he had lost his high range. "We never knew Marv had a high range," he said with a chuckle. He knew Marvin's deep voice well. For more than thirty-five years, he had been a loyal member of the bass section in the choir at the St. Paul Lutheran Church, a half-hour drive from his home in Forest Lake. Pastor Beebe also knew the spreading of his cancer and the effects of the medications were the real reasons he had wanted to stop singing in the choir. "But that's not something he would ever admit or talk about. If ever there was a classic, stoic Swede, it was Marv."

Pastor Beebe looked down at the family, seated below him in the front pews. His face grew solemn. "Marv's death is a freeing event," he said, "for himself, and in some ways for those of you who walked alongside him in his suffering."

Those of us who had walked alongside of him saw a life impaired by mental illness. But Marvin had not seen it that way. He took pride in Sharon and Kristi and their accomplishments. He battled the thistles in their lawn. After one of his many medical procedures, he worried about the temporary restriction on the weight he could lift—"Some sacks of flour weigh more than fifteen pounds!" He took satisfaction from his job at Cub Foods, working until the day before his final drive to the VA Medical Center.

Pastor Beebe folded up his notes and called Kristi to the pulpit.

She had slept little and eaten less in the three days since her father's death. While working on her tribute, she had sifted through albums and scrapbooks to find photographs for a picture board, worried about paying his taxes, and wondered what to do with his house.

She gripped the pages of her tribute with trembling hands as she looked out at the congregation and said, "I thought I would start with some stories from when I was young." She looked younger than her thirty years—too young to have decided to discontinue the treatments, to end the surgeries, to have planned her father's funeral.

Naomi passed a box of tissues down our pew. We had texted—"baggage 4 where r u"—as our children flew in from Philadelphia, Boston, and London. They shored me up with their love, willed me their fortitude. Now we willed our love and fortitude to Kristi, who looked small behind the large pulpit.

She offered her tribute in a soft, clear voice:

> Dad would listen to records in the evening. He would bring up a bunch of his 45s and listen to a couple stacks of them. He'd put a bunch on the record player, and it would drop them one by one and play the song with a bit of that scratching sound before the living room would fill with music.

I had not known my brother's daughter before the five days we spent together at the side of his hospital bed. I had been unaware of her attachment to her father, of her gentle wit, the resilience that resided behind her quiet smile.

I was surprised to learn of the many good memories she had, the times he gave her special gifts, and how he had put her favorite song, "The Lion Sleeps Tonight," on his record player every single night. I did not know about the two years between his layoff at Control Data and his job at Cub Foods when, free from the stress of work, he drove her to horseback riding lessons and bought inline skates so he could skate alongside of her.

I had only seen his illness.

She took a deep breath before continuing:

> Those are some good memories, but there were some very difficult times for my Dad and myself and our family and friends. It was a fact of his life just as much as anything else. He struggled hard with mental illness, and it caused hardship for himself and his friends and family.
>
> In the end, the mental illness did not win. When he got sick this final time, we all came together for him and held onto him tightly until the very end. The hardship and the cancer may have tried to drive us away in the past, but we could not be thwarted, and love and family and friendship triumphed.

In the end, when we all came together, I understood something I had not understood before. My brother's acts of defiance—refusing to acknowledge his mental illness, going off his medications, raging at my interventions—were marks of a courageous struggle. With a fierce determination, he had sought to live a life free from the stigma and constraints of mental illness.

Kristi looked out at the somber faces in the pews:

> But those are my so-called words of wisdom and
> reflection. I think it might be more appropriate to
> share what we heard from my Dad in his final days.
>
> Several times while we sat with him at the VA
> hospital, when he started to say something, we leaned
> in close, expecting to hear a profound end-of-life rev-
> elation or a request for some sort of specific care. But
> it was always some plain simple question.
>
> He wanted to know the temperature outside.
> He wanted to know the score for the Super Bowl on
> Sunday evening. He wanted to know if he could have
> some Coke to drink.
>
> So I will leave you with one of the final things I
> learned from my dad. Sometimes people aren't look-
> ing for deep, complicated, lengthy things from you.
> They just need a bit of simple information.

She had learned from her father something I had taken a lifetime
to understand. He had little interest in deep analytical discussions
about our growing up on the farm, the complex relationships in our
family, the impact of being a twin. He preferred to talk of plain and
straightforward things. I had expected him to be an extension of me,
to share my interests, my taste, my ambitions. Mom and Dad had
tried to make him into the person they wanted him to be.

So had I.

Kristi picked up her notes and stepped down from the pulpit. It
was my turn to speak.

In the Old Testament story, Jacob had fled to Mesopotamia, "the
land of the people of the east," to live in the house of his mother's
brother in order to escape the murderous rage of his twin, Esau. After
two decades of distant separation, despite intrigue and treachery and
a threat of death, Jacob returned to reconcile with his twin:

And Esau ran to meet him, and embraced him, and
fell on his neck, and kissed him: and they wept.
(Genesis 33:4)

How many themes from an ancient biblical twin-myth had our
family reenacted? "And Isaac loved Esau…but Rebekah loved Jacob."
Dad favored me and Mom favored Marvin. Like Rebekah, Mom
tried to collude with my twin, pitting us against each other. I escaped
to the east. My twin and I lived apart for decades. And yet, our powerful bond remained intact. Like Jacob, I had returned to reconcile
with my twin.

Marvin's breakdown had stopped me in my tracks. It pulled me
back into his life. When I sat in front of the nurse in the emergency
room at the Rice Memorial Hospital, I had no way of knowing his
illness had set me off on a journey that would take me back to examine our past and to rediscover my deep relationships with him and the
people I loved.

In the end, I had come to see that I was more than half of a whole.
I could have a full and satisfying life separate from my twin without
taking anything away from him.

I stepped up to the pulpit and looked out at the faces of my cousins—Margaret and Jerry, who had raced through the paths in the
pigweed with Marvin and me; Sheldon, who pieced together two tricycles for us to ride when there were none to be bought; Karen, who
that morning had driven four hours from Fargo and had yet to drive
four hours back. I looked at Marvin's friends, Bill and Sina, who had
continued their friendship with him after he and Sharon divorced. At
his coworkers from Cub Foods, at his manager, who said Marvin was
the "best worker I ever had."

I shared a few memories of plain and simple things. I talked about
Dad's bargain, "two for the price of one"; about the bill of forty-five
dollars for a nine-day stay of a mother and her two infants at the Rice
Memorial Hospital; of Marvin's love of the Two-Tone.

I ended by recounting the way I had tried, after Mom's death, to break through his Swedish stoicism.

"Marvin, you know I love you," I said, as we approached the end of a conversation.

Click. He hung up without saying goodbye.

The following week I tried again.

"Marvin, you know I love you."

Click.

Another call, another attempt.

"You know I love you."

"Yes," he had said, his voice sputtering with annoyance. "I *already* know that!"

I closed my eyes during the final hymn and thought about my last hours with my brother. After the chaplain at the VA Medical Center said it was time to say the things we wanted to say, we had gathered in, close to him, as he lay in his hospital bed.

In hushed voices, we spoke of what we carried in our hearts. Mark told him that he had enjoyed having a "big brother." Betty apologized for the times she had thought of him as a nuisance. George thanked him for their many conversations. Kristi asked to be forgiven for the times she had become irritated with him. Sharon spoke of her grief over their divorce.

I asked for time alone with my twin.

I wanted to tell my brother that I was sorry for being embarrassed by his tics and shrugs, for taking advantage of Dad's favoritism, for not wanting his mental illness to intrude on my life. But I wasn't able to say any of that.

"I'm sorry for not being a better sister," was all I could choke out.

The words had resounded in my heart for as long as I remembered. Why were they so difficult to say?

I leaned in, my cheek nearly brushing his, to hear his fading voice.

"Maybe I wasn't always such a great brother."

With the oxygen bubbling in the bottle behind us, we raced down the long rows of corn, tassels towering above our heads. We leaped from the top of the ladder and sank into the bin of cool, slippery flax. We climbed to the top of the hay in the haymow, spread our arms wide, and soared with the swallows.

End

SELECTED SOURCES

Ainslie, R. C. *The Psychology of Twinship*. Northvale, NJ: Jason Aronson, 1997.

Centennial Publication Committee of the Salem Mission Covenant Church. *Crowning a Century: Salem Covenant Church, 1871–1971*. Pennock, MN: Salem Mission Covenant Church, 1971.

Elliott, C., and W. B. Bradbury. "Just as I Am." Hymn. Public domain, 1849.

Hewitt, E. E., and E. D. Wilson. "When We All Get to Heaven." Hymn. Public domain, 1898.

Holmberg, K. A. "The Story of Agatha." Unpublished manuscript, 1936.

Holmberg, P. P., and E. M. Holmberg. Letters to relatives in Bollnäs, Sweden (translation). Unpublished raw data, 1882–1903.

The Holy Bible, King James Version. Cambridge Edition, 1769; King James Bible Online, 2020. www.kingjamesbibleonline.org.

Johnson, C. L. "The Descendants of Karl Jonsson Johnson." Unpublished raw data, 2005.

Johnson, H. A. Poem in memory of his half sister Emma. Unpublished material, 1900.

Johnson, R. G. "Johnson Family History." Unpublished raw data, 1996.

Lawson, V. E., and J. E. Nelson. *Illustrated History and Descriptive and Biographical Review of Kandiyohi County, Minnesota*. St. Paul: Pioneer Press, 1905.

Lindholm, K. E., ed. "Holmberg Centennial: Commemorating 100 years of Per and Karin Holmberg and Their Descendants in America, 1882–1982." Unpublished manuscript, 1982.

Peterson, K. P. Tribute to her father, Marvin W. Peterson. Unpublished raw data, 2008.

Peterson, R. E. "Maria and Hjalmar's Family." Unpublished raw data, 1994.

Peterson, R. E. Multiple letters. Unpublished raw data, 1959–2000.

Peterson, S. C. "A Synopsis of Marv's Illness and Our Lives for Last 8 Mos." Unpublished raw data, 1987.

Peterson, T. B. "Research of Genealogy of Ola Pettersson." Unpublished raw data, 2015.

Peterson, W. G. "Family History." Unpublished raw data, 1977.

Sandell, C. "Day by Day." Hymn. Public domain, 1865.

Swift County Historical Society. *Swift County, Minnesota: A Collection of Historical Sketches and Family Histories.* Dallas: Taylor Publishing, 1980.

ACKNOWLEDGMENTS

I am grateful to the many people who supported and assisted me in the writing and publishing of this book:

A special thanks to my mother, Ruby Peterson[†], for her prolific writing of letters and her recording of family stories, which provided much of the material; to my twin, Marvin Peterson[†], for his courage in striving to live a normal life in spite of being encumbered with a mental illness, knowing he would never have forgiven me for writing about him; to my sister, Betty Oberg, for always standing up for me and for speaking the truth when I most needed to hear it; to my brother, Mark Peterson, for answering my many questions about our family farm, which he still farms.

I thank my children, Naomi Haus-Roth, Nikolaus Bates-Haus, and Stephanie Schorge, for their insight and assistance, their unflagging support, and at those times when I was most discouraged, keeping me from incinerating my manuscript. I thank my son-in-law, Kevin Roth, and my daughter-in-law, Lissie Bates-Haus, for being advocates for my book.

A heartfelt appreciation to my twin's ex-wife, Sharon Peterson, who provided some of the material for this book, and to their daughter, Kristi Peterson, for her gracious acceptance of my writing about her father, and to both of them for loving my twin in spite of his struggle with bipolar disorder.

I'm indebted to my psychotherapist, Dr. Paul Lippmann, for his compassion and insight, for helping me break free of the anchors from my past, and for showing me that my dreams were a window into my unconscious mind.

I'll forever be thankful for my dear friend and teacher, Michelle Gillett[†], who inspired me to write and encouraged me to compile my stories into a manuscript; for my editors, Nina Ryan, who helped me sleuth out my themes and shape my narrative, and Rachel Urquhart, who helped me sculpt my book and who continues to be a perceptive and supportive writing teacher.

I can't say enough about the invaluable coaching and driving force of my agent, Alexis Hurley, without whom my book would never have gotten out in the world; about the unfailingly collaborative team at Post Hill Press, Debby Englander, Heather King, and Katie Reid; about Kim Dower, an unstoppable force.

I'm grateful for my cousins, Tom Peterson, who spent an entire winter gathering information about our Pettersson great-grand-parents; Karen Lindholm Horsley, who put together a book about our Holmberg great-grandparents, including original letters written during their emigration; Corrine Johnson[†] and Bob Johnson[†], who did genealogical research about our Jonsson great-grandparents.

I'm thankful for my readers' group—Susanne King, Maggie Howard[†], Wendy Holmes, Sarah Ginocchio, Barney Edmonds, Leslie Bedford—who provided honest feedback along the way; Frank Simmons[†], for his early support and guidance; Judy Miller, for push-ing me to write down the farm stories I loved to tell; Rich Berlin, for counseling patience; those who gave me feedback on earlier versions of my book—Joan Kavanaugh, David Bruce, Gerry Hurley, Laura Flint, Jane Bloom, John Kavanaugh, Diane Johnson, Jean Forbord, David Smith[†]—and many others who encouraged me along the way (my apologies to those I've left out).

Above all, I thank my husband, George, for his support and uncomplaining tolerance of the hours, weeks, and years I spent writ-ing this book, turning off his favorite classical music radio station so I could have a quiet space to write.

[†] deceased

ABOUT THE AUTHOR

Author Photo by Edward Acker, Photographer

Marilyn Peterson Haus grew up on a Minnesota farm. Having retired from a business career, she enjoys gardening, cross country skiing, and listening to classical music. She lives with her husband in the beautiful Berkshire Hills in Massachusetts.